Gifts of Wisdom

PRACTICES FOR HEALING AND EMPOWERMENT

DAVID D McLEOD

Featuring: Frank Byrum, Laura Di Franco, Ilene L. Dillon, Susan Ernst, Virginia Rounds Griffiths, Mary Jo Halligan, Steve Halligan, R. Scott Holmes, Sara Jane, Denyse LeFever, Michol Mae, Ricki McKenna, Laurie Morin, Laina Orlando, Carol Pilkington, Janine Savient, Bonnie Sheldon, Gwenda Smith, Jennifer K. Sproul, Janette Stuart, Star Studonivic

PRACTICES FOR HEALING AND EMPOWERMENT

DAVID D McLEOD

Featuring: Frank Byrum, Laura Di Franco, Ilene L. Dillon, Susan Ernst, Virginia Rounds Griffiths, Mary Jo Halligan, Steve Halligan, R. Scott Holmes, Sara Jane, Denyse LeFever, Michol Mae, Ricki McKenna, Laurie Morin, Laina Orlando, Carol Pilkington, Janine Savient, Bonnie Sheldon, Gwenda Smith, Jennifer K. Sproul, Janette Stuart, Star Studonivic

Gifts of Wisdom

Practices for Healing and Empowerment

Copyright ©2024 David D McLeod, DD, PhD, CMLC

Published by Brave Healer Productions

Designed by Dino Marino Design, dinomarinodesign.com

eBook ISBN: 978-1-961493-38-4

Paperback ISBN: 978-1-961493-39-1

"The authors of *Gifts of Wisdom* have created a sacred space for the Reader, amplifying the potential for healing and soul evolution. I especially love the reach of this book, beckoning the Reader to explore the tragic and transformative and emphasizing the celebration of life's journey wherever one finds oneself on this path. Each chapter offers a powerful story and a clearly delineated practice that challenges the Reader to look at experiences from a new perspective, like seeing the gift and possibility for growth that rests in the harrowing and even the heartbreaking. Reach beyond limitation and embrace new horizons through the words of these inspired authors!"

~ **Elizabeth R. Kipp**,
Stress Management and Historical Trauma Specialist, Bestselling author of The Way Through Chronic Pain: Tools to Reclaim Your Healing Power

"What took decades to refine is now ours to grow from. What an honour it is to read this book and to realize the depth of significant support and healing that can come from older adults around us. In a world where our elders are often unheard or even unseen, sometimes even by themselves, this book is an expression of the respect and the reverence that, as a society, we can show them, thereby learning so much more about ourselves, our families, our communities and living a peaceful, healing existence. *Gifts of Wisdom* is shifting the lens of who becomes the teacher, and the transformational stories are alive on these pages."

~ **Dianna Leeder CPCC**, *Intuitive Coach for the Voiceless, Best-Selling author of the series Find Your Voice, Save Your Life*

"The stories in this collection share pearls of wisdom, sometimes raw, like broken shards pointing to our own unresolved wounds. The *Gifts of Wisdom* stories inspire our own hero's or shero's journey inward. The wisdom guides us to allow our wise adult self to rescue our wounded inner child, summon curiosity, ask tough questions, and learn to forgive—ourselves and others. I especially appreciated the pearls of body wisdom woven into the stories. This is a guidebook to savor with a journal and pen in hand to claim and embody your own gifts of inner wisdom."

~ **Leah Skurdal, MA**, *Resilience Guide and COO at The Wellness Universe*

"*Gifts of Wisdom: Practices for Healing and Empowerment* is not just another supportive inspirational book with life stories offering practical life tips and advice. It is powerful, nourishing food supporting a deep soul awakening along with spiritual growth. I felt as if the stories I was drawn to read initially were written just for me and my own life journey. Powerful! What followed was the release of my current of emotional energy bubbling up from the stories shared from the heart space of each author. The helpful life advice shared in *The Practice* is easy to understand and implement. This is a well-rounded book, a gift first to yourself and one you will want to share wholeheartedly with others."

~ **Nancy Stevens**, *Coach, Vibrant Well-Being Host, Best-selling Author*

"Reading *Gifts of Wisdom* feels like a hug from my grandma. As a child, my favorite part of summer was visiting her and asking questions about life, plants, animals, and nature. She was kind and knowledgeable, imparting wisdom in a way that made sense to my level of understanding at each stage of life. My philosophy of life and love was learned roaming the woods and her gardens, asking her questions, and deeply listening to her answers. Grandma taught by example, walking her talk, telling stories as illustrations, and being a good model.

The *Gifts of Wisdom* book has the same energy. The stories are rich and clearly lead the reader on a path of wisdom and knowledge. Each chapter is filled with brilliant information shared in a clear, caring way. The authors show that they are experts in their chosen field and lovingly share their journey to wisdom. The tools at the end of each chapter are an additional gift with step-by-step instructions for healing and releasing. This book answers questions I didn't know to ask and clarifies what I already know. It truly is a gift from each author!"

~ **Carolyn McGee**, *Living Inspired Expert*

"Nothing touches your heart like a story that nudges the resonance of "I felt that too!" This book is filled with lifetimes of living, learning, practices, and wisdom. Each author shares their story with such deep authenticity and vulnerability that I felt immediate connection with their story and learning journey. The practices shared have such practical application to daily life. When wisdom speaks, it is time to listen."

~ **Sharon Carne**,
Director of Training and Program Development, Sound Wellness Institute

"When we look around at people who have gray hair, who have some wrinkles and look like they've seen a thing or two, we're absolutely right: they've seen a thing or two—or three—and they're still here because they've developed some resilience, because they've learned from their experiences. If we pause long enough to listen, we can learn something, too.

In this powerful book, *Gifts of Wisdom*, David McLeod and 21 other authors bravely and powerfully share their stories of healing and transformation. In the face of different and taxing circumstances, each author found a way to move through their situation, and each one emerged more humble, wiser, and more relatable as a result.

What I find extraordinary about this book is its practical orientation. Each chapter contains both the author's story and a specifically delineated practice we can all work on. We learn best through practical application, and each author generously provides us with a practice that has worked for them. These practices can work for us, too.

So many of us stop short on a transformational or healing journey because we feel we're all alone. We are not alone, and this book proves it. I invite you to delve into these stories and come away knowing that you, too, can learn and grow through just about anything. Here's to your transformation!"

~ **Rev. Tomás Garza**, *A Course In Miracles Instructor, Bestselling Author*

"The profound journeys of self-discovery and growth in *Gifts of Wisdom* invite readers to explore the nuanced interplay between experience and discernment. Personal and universal themes coupled with reflective and introspective narratives ignite deep contemplation about the true essence of wisdom. Through a blend of unique anecdotes and spiritual insights, authors offer a rich tapestry of stories and practices aimed at unlocking and embracing one's inner wisdom.

Each chapter is a quest for knowledge and a heartfelt endeavor to share the transformative power of wisdom gleaned from diverse experiences. *Gifts of Wisdom* is a compelling invitation to embrace the wisdom that comes with experience, challenge societal notions and norms, and find fulfillment through a deeper connection with one's inner self."

~ **Gayle Nowak**, *Communications and Emotional Wellness Coach, Founder of The Story Stylist LLC*

"I love hearing people tell their story. If the storyteller is someone I know personally, the story adds another layer of interest about that person, and I relish the opportunity to know them better, and curiosity compels me to actively listen to every detail. When the person is unknown to me, I want to learn what it was that created the person they became.

What I did not expect from each story was the recognition of some small part of me that related to/resonated with each person's journey. *Gifts of Wisdom* is a wonderful compilation of what we humans face in life. The stories are warm, happy, sad, and real. And the cherry on the sundae is the "gift of the wisdom" to be found in the *Practice* each writer used to become the hero of their story.

To me, experience is living life, and the wisdom is what results from the experiences of living. Dive into the glorious wisdom that resulted from each author's experience and find the bit of yourself that connects you with the storyteller."

~ **Diane Boyko Achatz**, *TCM Master Coach and Diabetic Lifestyle Coach*

To all brave souls who face the shadows of life's challenges,

To all those who succeed and all those who fail,

To all adventurers who stumble and rise, only to embrace
their scars as symbols of survival and strength,

To all seekers, healers, and warriors of the heart who greet adversity
with courage, weather the storms and emerge with gifts of wisdom,

This book is for you. Your perseverance and hope in the face
of despair, along with your commitment to
growth and healing, are the true essence of its words.

May these pages honor your struggles, celebrate your achievements,
and bring you healing and empowerment from the shared stories
and practices within. May the wisdom in this collection be a beacon
of light in your darkest moments, a source of solace
and inspiration as you continue your journey

SEEDS OF WISDOM

in the dark silence where i fell,
the trees were tall and still
like soldiers holding ground,
standing steadfast and ready
for an enemy that stopped attacking eons ago

my heart throbbed,
flushing my ears
with a rush of blood that moved so fast
it seemed to suck all the air out of the forest

sun vectors cascaded through leaves
around pine cones
between branches
looking for a pool to settle in

finding only my prone body,
they settled there,
swimming and dancing on my skin,
planting Seeds of Wisdom in the spaces
between my heart and my soul

~ David D McLeod

Foreword

Anna Pereira

Founder and CEO, The Wellness Universe, International Bestselling Author

For as long as I can remember, people have sought my opinion, advice, and guidance. Even as a teenager, I was often told I was wise beyond my years—a statement I didn't fully grasp at the time, though I found myself surrounded by older friends, teachers, guidance counselors, and even my friends' parents. As I grew and embarked on various entrepreneurial endeavors, particularly in the fashion industry, this wisdom continued to shine through. I vividly recall a moment when I was explaining my clothing line to a buyer, and they asked if I was a motivational speaker. At that time, I didn't even know what a motivational speaker was! The truth is, I hadn't yet embraced the wisdom that others saw in me.

Over the past decade, I've dedicated myself to the world of transformation and self-care, founding and leading The Wellness Universe as its CEO. This journey is what led me to cross paths with David McLeod, a remarkable individual who has become both a colleague and a friend. For several years, I've had the privilege of working closely with David, witnessing firsthand the profound impact of his wisdom and the transformative tools he shares. While his approach may appeal to different people in different ways, beneath his style lies a heart of GOLD, with a purpose driven by a deep desire to make the world a better place.

David has dedicated the fabric of his being to making the world a better place. He is a man who stands in his truth and believes this is what we all must do—live from our truth. He is unwavering in this being the key to living our best life, so of course Gifts of Wisdom could only be birthed by him.

Wisdom, in my view, is cultivated through a blend of experience, reflection, learning, and the thoughtful application of knowledge. David exemplifies this beautifully, combining his rich experiences with a visionary outlook for humanity—one where happiness, health, and healing are attainable for all. This book is a testament to that vision, bringing together some of the brightest minds, stories, and tools, all rooted in wisdom. The narratives within these pages are penned by sage guides, and David has masterfully curated the ultimate team of authors and teachers, offering us an invaluable resource for personal growth and transformation.

Through this book, David not only shares his incredible journey but also introduces us to a community of light bringers and healers. These individuals, through their wisdom, take us on a journey to uncover, discover, and recover the parts of ourselves that can truly be transformed. David has gifted us with this treasury of wisdom, and I believe this book has the power to profoundly change your life.

I know David and all the authors are here and awaiting to connect with you. Use this book as your reference, inspiration and connect with the wise teachers within.

DISCLAIMER

This book is designed to provide competent, reliable, and educational information regarding health, wellness, nutrition, and/or business and other subject matter. However, it is sold with the understanding the authors and publisher specifically disclaim all responsibility for any liability, loss, or risk, personal or otherwise, incurred as a consequence, directly or indirectly, of the use and application of any of the contents of this publication.

In order to maintain the anonymity of others, some names and identifying characteristics of people, places, and organizations described in this book have been changed.

This publication contains content that may be potentially triggering or disturbing. Individuals who are sensitive to certain themes are advised to exercise caution while reading.

The opinions, ideas, and recommendations contained in this publication do not necessarily represent those of the publisher. The use of any information provided in this book is solely at your own risk.

Our authors represent cultures worldwide and as such, there may be differences in language and expressions. As a global publisher, we have made the conscious choice to not edit these nuances so each chapter is authentic and in its author's words.

Know that the experts here have shared their tools, practices, and knowledge with you with a sincere and generous intent to assist you on your journey. Please contact them with any questions you may have about the techniques or information they provided. They will be happy to assist you further and be an ongoing resource for your success!

Table of Contents

Introduction

"What's the difference between experience and wisdom?"

Professor Coleman, my second-year English literature teacher, was a curious little man—some might even use the word "strange." Somewhere in his mid-30s, he struck me as a wise old man in a young man's body.

He stood at the front of the class, his round, brown-rimmed glasses tight against his forehead as if he had glued them there. A wavy tuft of walnut hair curled back from his receding hairline and seemed to pull his mouth up into a tight smile.

His left hand clutched Beowulf tight to his chest, a clear sign of his reverence for this epic poem that hardly anybody in the class understood. His shoes slapped the floor as he paced in front of the podium, glancing occasionally in the direction of the 20 of us who had begrudgingly agreed to attend his class. When he ambled to the left, I could see a hint of elbow peeking through a small hole in the sleeve patch of his faded navy jacket. He seemed oblivious or distracted, and his burgundy bow tie was forever tilted at the throat of his crumpled white shirt.

"Well…?"

He paused for a moment, scanning the class as if beseeching the ether.

"Well…?"

His voice drifted as he resumed pacing.

Fisher, a row ahead of me, was the first to venture an opinion. "I guess they both have to do with acquired knowledge," he offered.

In military college, rules were sacrosanct, so I attended all my classes as required. However, nothing in the code of conduct obligated me to pay attention. Coleman's quiet demeanor usually just put me to sleep—a proposition further facilitated by my desk choice near the back of the classroom. Today was no different. The conversation initiated by Fisher soon faded into my mental haze, and I have no further recollection of it.

It turned out, however, that Coleman's question tumbled like a thistle seed into a crevice in my brain. Over the next few days, it sprouted and grew, and I became hypnotized by it, pushing myself to conjure a satisfying response. Since we had been studying Beowulf, it seemed fitting that my answer should model the story's poetic nature—though I was loath to attempt an *Olde Englishe* version. This is what I came up with:

Experience is knowledge with scar tissue.

Wisdom is knowledge with wrinkles.

Although I never shared this clever bumper sticker aphorism in public before today, it has simmered in my subconscious for perhaps 50 years, shaping and guiding my understanding of both experience and wisdom. It wasn't until I had the idea to write this book that the phrase resurfaced in my memory.

But, in the interim, it turned out that my perspective had shifted.

In March of 2023, I completed my 70th transit around the sun, and—no surprise—the subject of aging and elderhood began to rise in my awareness.

Am I old now? I don't feel old! I certainly don't feel wise...

Maybe it's time for me to grow up.

Maybe it's time for me to embrace my inner elder.

Maybe it's time for me to start acting like a grandfather or a shaman...

Thoughts like these persisted for a couple of months, and I realized that I was resisting the idea of growing old—as if aging was some form of leprosy that required my incarceration in a vile institution where I would eventually be forgotten.

I set out to do some meditation, introspection, and journaling about this, and in the process, some optimistic thoughts began to appear.

Age is only a number; no need to avoid it.

I am still young at heart, regardless of how my body might feel.

In my own way, I have accumulated a lot of wisdom—it's time to acknowledge and accept it—and, of course, share it.

In the midst of these thoughts, there were still some diminishing mental echoes: *Fraud! Poser!*

Silence! I commanded. *I'm going to write a book about wisdom, no matter what you might say about it.*

It was a spontaneous idea, writing a book. *Where did that come from?*

My body stiffened. My heart pounded. My stomach wobbled.

Palpable clenches of fear signaled it was a good choice for me, and once the decision was firm in my mind, fear began to dissipate. Within a few days, I once again heard the singing in my heart. Energy moved through me, and the honey-sweet warmth of joy replenished me.

This is the nature of passion—an elixir that powers the engine of my soul.

For this project, my intuition insisted on collaboration. Right away, I wanted to invite all my elder friends and encourage them to share their wisdom for the next generations. Indeed, my initial title was *Elder Wisdom*, and while that felt right—intellectually speaking—my spiritual essence was lukewarm about it.

This was about the time I began remembering Professor Coleman's question and the idea it had brought forth for me so long ago. As I continued inviting people to participate in my project, a new thought appeared:

You don't have to have white hair or wrinkles to be wise.

Of course not! Such an obvious statement, now that I think about it.

At the same time, I also began to recognize that wisdom and experience are cozy dance partners. While I believe we all have access to accumulated wisdom that doesn't require a particular individual experience, for the most part, it seems that we experience things in our life journey that lead us to learn and grow—*and* acquire wisdom in the bargain. In other words, for most of us, most of the time, wisdom emanates out of our experiences. But there is no minimum age for when this wisdom can arrive.

Thus, I stopped looking for elders and began instead looking for wellness and healing practitioners with a deep connection to their inner sage.

The Universe certainly provided!

After several months and about 45 interviews with potential candidates, I assembled an incredible team of authors, all of whom resonated with my vision to share vulnerable stories and powerful practices. Each of these wonderful and delightful people brings forth undeniable wisdom with gentle grace. And their stories are relatable and inspirational—even though the circumstances in some cases may seem severely unpleasant.

You are in for a real treat, dear reader, as you'll not find a more compelling collection of stories and practices anywhere.

I invite you to choose a sacred space and a comfortable chair. Turn off your phone and any other source of potential interruption. Give yourself permission to become fully present to the incredible *Gifts of Wisdom* you'll find in this treasure chest.

Immerse yourself in the stories. Get to know the authors. Take advantage of the practices. Heal and grow.

Embrace your own inner wisdom.

CHAPTER 1

What Irks You?

HOW TO TRANSFORM FRUSTRATION INTO FULFILLMENT

David D McLeod, DD, PhD, Certified Master Life Coach

MY STORY

PROVING MY WORTH

I'm sick and tired of living according to other people's expectations. Why can't I just be me?

When do I get my chance to have what I want?

I followed all the rules—where is the happiness and success I worked for?

When will I ever be deemed good enough?

In 1991, uninvited thoughts like these began to distract me. I was two years away from my 40th birthday, and now the idea of a *mid-life crisis* was looming large. I couldn't bear the thought of becoming another 40-something statistic, so, like the *good little boy* I had dutifully and faithfully embodied, I crammed these ideas into my inner vault. No way I'd give them a single moment of airplay!

Still, I believed I needed to demonstrate my worthiness.

I was working as a software developer for a small company without receiving the recognition—or the pay—I believed I deserved. It had been a struggle to land this job: my background *wasn't deep enough,* my education *wasn't focused enough*. As a result, I was hired at a lower salary than normal for the kind of work I was doing. The quality of my work was never in question; I always delivered everything expected of me—and more. But there was always a nagging belief that I wasn't quite good enough. How could I prove my worth once and for all?

Credentials. That's what you need!

I enrolled in a master's program at the University of Alberta. A surprising sense of urgency grew within me: somehow, I'd have to complete this program as quickly as possible. This meant quitting my job and attending classes full-time.

I started in earnest in the first semester of 1992, and I graduated—*cum laude*—in 1994 with a Master of Computer Science degree. My grades were so good that I received an enthusiastic invitation to continue as a PhD candidate. Naturally, my ego-mind danced with delight at such an opportunity—*even more credibility!*— so I embarked on a secondary journey in Computer Science theory that ended in mid-1995 after I completed all the coursework and only a fraction of the dissertation research.

What happened? The explanation requires some backtracking.

MOM'S REVELATION

In May 1992—Mother's Day weekend, to be precise—my mom assembled the family to reveal some dire news. She had been diagnosed with stage four breast cancer that had already metastasized in her lymph nodes. She would be going into Misericordia Hospital right away for what was euphemistically termed "palliative care." I hadn't heard that phrase before, but I soon learned it meant she wouldn't be leaving the hospital alive.

For the next three weeks, I spent my days attending university classes and my evenings sitting with Mom in the hospital. For the first of those weeks, she was lucid and conversational. I remember us watching *A Fish Called Wanda* in her room one night. I just reveled in Mom's contagious laughter—even while wincing at the pain in her chest. Her condition deteriorated during the next few days, and her lucidity faded. By the eighth or ninth day, the doctor prescribed intravenous morphine to dull her pain—as well as her consciousness. From that point forward, Mom was almost comatose, although there were moments when her eyes flashed open. I convinced myself she still recognized me.

On June 2, 1992, I held Mom's hand as she opened her eyes for one more look before taking her last breath. Not the way she would've wanted to be remembered, no doubt. She would've much preferred to be dressed to the nines at a party, dancing her pretty figure among all her friends, cavorting like the free spirit she had been for all of my life, and then just dropping dead with a big smile on her face.

One of Mom's last commands to me was "Don't be maudlin, David."

She spoke these words on that day three weeks earlier when she broke the news about her condition. I wasn't sure exactly what she meant, but I took it as a requirement to maintain my trained attitude of stoicism at all costs. Of course, I accommodated her wishes during that final long exhale—and well beyond: there were no tears; she would've been proud.

Although I felt sad about Mom's passing, the primary energy I experienced was inexplicable relief, as if a straitjacket had been removed and I could breathe again. Strange: up till that point, I had never noticed constricted breathing.

A few weeks later, my world flipped into emotional chaos.

A BIG WAKE-UP

"Hello?" she called. The door slammed behind her. "It's me!" My sister Diane and her daughter Bayley—unexpected visitors.

I looked up from the cutting board as she turned into the kitchen. "Hey, Di, what's up?"

"Bayley and I were heading home, and I just felt like checking in."

"Everything good here." I tilted my glass and took a swig. "Care for a martini? Glass of wine?"

"No," she said, "We're not staying. I just had something on my mind, and I wanted to talk to you."

Uh-oh, I thought. I regarded her with curiosity and dread, waiting for her to speak.

She blurted, "It's been three weeks since Mom's funeral, and I still haven't seen any emotion or tears from you. What the hell is wrong with you?"

My throat started burning as if a pressurized bottle of acid had burst within me. In the next moment, Diane was up against the wall, my right hand around her neck. In my racing mind, a thought screamed: *Don't you tell me how to grieve!* But what seethed out of my mouth was, "Don't you tell me how to BE!"

Diane was so stunned she hung motionless, gaping at me with wide eyes and open mouth. Another part of my mind wondered: *How did this happen?* Then, complete silence, except for a distinct mental whisper: *Enough. Time to let go.*

Silence gave way to a strange wind rushing through my head. I regained awareness of the situation and released my hand. I shook my head absently and muttered, "Sorry, I don't know what…" My voice trailed off. Shame and horror rose in my chest to replace the overflowing acid.

Diane's face explored various expressions, settling on righteous indignation. Her body tensed, she glared at me, and half-whispered-half-shouted: "How *dare* you!"

I was confused and disoriented. My body started shaking. Diane was clearly yelling other stuff at me, but nothing was getting through; I had mentally checked out.

Somehow, I ended up wandering barefoot around the neighborhood. I replayed the scene in my mind multiple times, trying to understand my outburst. The dreadful realization dawned on me that my daughter, my son, and my niece had all witnessed my conniption. I cringed at the faint mental echoes of my daughter's plea: "Daddy, don't!"

By the time I ventured home, Diane and Bayley were gone. So were my wife and children. I was left to stew in my toxic juices.

According to McLeod family dynamics back then, no one ever discussed this event—at least not around me—as if my tantrum had never happened. Indeed, I banished it from memory for years.

CHAOS INTENSIFIES

One thing became clear: although Diane had hurled all that judgment on me, it was Mom's voice I was hearing. It was my mother I tried to silence, not my sister.

This wake-up call stirred up a whirlwind of memory sound-bites—mostly Mom's *irrefutable motherisms*—random fragments of which swirled without context like hungry piranha in the river of my awareness:

Children are to be seen and not heard.

Don't do as I do, do as I say.

Forget about being a musician. You have to find a real job instead.

I'm your mother. You're supposed to listen to me.

Be a good boy. Do as you're told.

I know you better than you know yourself.

The incessant swirl became frantic. I was desperate to shut everything out of my mind. I found partial relief in the depths of many martini glasses, but the hangovers became unbearable. To return to some form of *normal*, I buried myself in my studies, but the sense of urgency remained. In fact, it grew stronger.

That invisible straitjacket had apparently dammed up more than I could've imagined—now that it had been released, repercussions rippled within me for three more years. Answerless questions plagued me:

Whatever happened to the real me?

How long must I continue the charade of showing up how people expect me to?

How do I make this nightmare stop?

Obviously, I needed help. But I knew nothing about psychotherapy, and my attempts to get support from friends, family, and church only intensified my negative belief that I was the evil one here. Part of me wanted to end it all.

Eventually, I concluded that the support I sought was not available to me in Edmonton, so in 1995, I made a radical and impetuous—if reluctant—decision to change everything all at once. I terminated my PhD program, announced to my wife that I wanted a divorce, found a software engineering job in Silicon Valley, and left my family. In short, I fled what I believed was eating away at me from the inside out.

Alas, my frustration, resentment, and anger didn't simply disappear because of a change in scenery. Indeed, shortly after arriving in Palo Alto, I began to experience severe depression that led to dark thoughts of suicide;

it was only the bleak prospect of rendering my beloved children fatherless that stayed my hand.

HEALING AND INTEGRATING

My escape to California revealed itself as one of the best unconscious decisions of my life. Serendipity connected me with many resources that helped me uncover and heal hidden wounds that had spawned so much pain and misery within me over all those years. The most profound healing and awakening came during a life-changing weekend in May 2003 when I attended a *New Warrior Training Adventure.*

As men stepped one-by-one onto *The Sacred Carpet*, I became mesmerized. Each man took center stage, did some incredible healing work, and then, about 20 to 30 minutes later, marched off completely transformed. To call it *inspiring* would hardly do it justice.

Finally, my turn came.

I stood in the center, the other men surrounding me in a perimeter of guardians. My body buzzed in anticipation.

A facilitator appeared in front of me, and the men around the circle faded out of my awareness. He was a masterful guide, and I trusted him like I trusted no one before. He asked questions to establish context, but their only real purpose was to induce me to unlock emotions inside that I had kept hidden away for so long.

Then it happened: the dormant volcano within me erupted, and hot, blood-red rage spewed out of me.

Screaming.

Cursing.

Raving.

A tennis racket magically appeared in my palm, which served as a battering ram to massacre a pile of pillows in front of me. But I did not see pillows! I saw Mother, Father, bosses, associates, priests, leaders, and yes, even God, all of whom I had unconsciously been blaming for the deplorable state of my life. I pounded and raged until I had no more strength, until my voice was a hoarse whisper, until my breath was spent, until my inner volcano was empty.

I vaguely remember croaking, "I just want someone to love me for who I am."

From out of nowhere, a man came to my side to assume the role of *Ideal Mom*; he held me in the most loving way I could've ever imagined.

Tears flooded out of me. My body shivered and shook with uncontrollable sobbing. *Ideal Mom* repeated phrases like "I love you so much" and "You are my amazing and beautiful boy." So much junk came out of my nose, eyes, and mouth I couldn't believe it! Who would've expected a 50-year old man to fall apart this way?

Eventually, the deluge subsided, and I melted into *Ideal Mom*'s arms. I was drained like a sponge squeezed bone-dry, and yet there was an unfamiliar, profound peace within me. When I summoned the strength to stand, a surge of warm gold-blue light blossomed into my heart. I put my hands on my chest and smiled softly and effortlessly. I couldn't believe how amazing and alive I felt.

The facilitator beamed as he stepped back in front of me.

"What is true about you right now, David, in this moment?"

Despite my raspy throat, I managed to declare, "I am a divine being of boundless light and love, and I'm here to make the world a better place for everyone."

The men around the carpet burst into cheering and applause. Delicious gratitude flowed into my heart; fresh warm tears trickled down my cheeks.

As I scanned my ring of guardians, their faces and bodies faded like mist, and all I could see were bright gold-blue waves of honeysuckle energy moving back and forth among us all. In that moment, I knew the true meaning of *We Are All One*.

The love I felt for everyone was immense, beyond my capacity to contain. And for the first time in memory, I felt this love directed at myself too. What a gift!

I made several silent vows that day:

I will never again hide my feelings or my truth.

I will never again suppress my own wants and needs just to fulfill the needs of others.

No matter what happens in my life from now on, I will never again deny who I am in order to please anyone else.

Little did I know that this was just the beginning of true fulfillment for me.

THE PRACTICE

I have learned that I'm blessed with deep internal desires that emanate out of my true *Spiritual Nature*. However, as a member of humanity, I'm also blessed with a powerful ego-mind that helps me navigate safely through the physical world. I believe this soul/ego-mind relationship is much the same for all normal human beings.

Frustration is a state of being that arises from unmet expectations, obstacles, or perceived failures. It happens when a strong desire or goal is thwarted by a force that is often deemed to be external.

Emotionally, frustration manifests as a combination of sadness, fear, and anger. Physically, it may show up as tightness in the body, which is why the body has a natural tendency to invoke strong movements to *fight it off*.

Here is a process I use nowadays to deal with frustration and find my way back to fulfillment.

CREATE A SAFE SPACE

As soon as you become aware of frustration within you, find a quiet and safe space where you can express yourself fully. Keep a journal and pen handy.

ACKNOWLEDGE AND FEEL

Give yourself permission to embrace and experience all the feelings and sensations in your body. Move, shake, dance, jump, stomp, clap—whatever allows your body to express the energy safely. Allow the intensity of the energy to rise to a maximum and use the power of your voice to facilitate its release.

INQUIRE WITHIN

After the energy dissipates, sit down with your journal. Contemplate and answer the following questions.

1. What do I want that is not coming to me?

2. Who or what is preventing me from having it?

3. What happens in my body when I am kept from what I want?

4. What stories appear in my mind when my desire is denied or thwarted?

5. What judgments do I have about the situation? About myself?

FORGIVE

There's a chance you identified someone external as the cause of your frustration. Understand that this person's actions were all about him or her and had nothing to do with you. Can you bring yourself to forgive this person and relieve yourself of notions of revenge or justice?

And what about you? Can you forgive yourself for all the things you imagine you did wrong to allow this frustration into your life?

Forgiveness is a real powerhouse for returning to fulfillment. Take advantage of it.

THE REAL CULPRIT

When you experience frustration, it's usually because your ego-mind is attempting to overpower a calling of your soul. Because its own existence depends on controlling everything, your ego-mind demands full attention. Therefore, it will do whatever it must do—including deceiving and lying to you—to keep you disconnected from your true nature.

Initiate a meditative open dialog with your ego-mind. Find out what danger it perceives that it's trying to prevent. Remind your ego-mind that you're now an adult and that you're capable of making healthy choices for yourself. Firmly assume control of your life and invite your ego-mind to support you as a co-pilot rather than trying to co-opt your sovereignty as captain of your own ship.

EXPRESS GRATITUDE

Remember, your ego-mind is the true enemy of your fulfillment. However, it's really trying to be helpful in its own dysfunctional way, so give thanks for its intention to keep you safe.

When that is done, express gratitude to your concept of a *Higher Power* for bringing into your life what you truly desire and for empowering you to experience and express all of who you really are in every moment.

After all, isn't that the true meaning of fulfillment?

Find out more about David in the About **David D McLeod** section at the end of the book.

https://YourLifeMasteryCoach.com

CHAPTER 2

Break Out the Good China

CULTIVATING CREATIVITY IN DAILY LIFE

Laurie Morin

"You can't use up creativity.
The more you use, the more you have."

~ Maya Angelou

Have you ever told yourself that you're not creative?

Many of us learned that story as children when the educational system categorized us as brainy, athletic, artistic, musical, or socially gifted.

In elementary school, I was labeled as a shy brainiac, and I believed it. As an analytical, left-brained law professor, I thought creativity was reserved for people with a special, divinely bestowed gift for art, music, or literature. It was not for people like me, who were so bad at art, that I got my first "D" from my fifth-grade teacher.

Many years later, my mother told me Ms. Bean gave me a D in art to show me that I wasn't perfect. But the damage was done. I spent most of my life believing creativity was reserved for more talented people.

The gift of wisdom I learned much later in life is that everyone is creative. It's not a special gift bestowed on a select few. It's our birthright as human beings with free will and imagination to create the story of our lives.

The best part is that we have multiple ways of expressing our creativity. The more we pursue one creative outlet, the more creativity we find in other areas of our lives.

This insight literally changed my life. I now see creativity everywhere and use my imagination to create a more beautiful life. When you start flexing your creative muscles, your life becomes a masterpiece in the making.

MY STORY

My journey to a more creative life started during the pandemic. I retired and was bored, stuck in a new home in a strange city with no friends and no job to occupy my day.

Our new house had a cement slab smack dab in the middle of the small yard, disconnected from everything. It reminded me of the Joni Mitchell song about paving paradise to put up a parking lot. So, I decided to build a flagstone path connecting the cement slab to the back steps, transforming it into a walkway that led to the garden.

This project was an aberration from my usual desk job. I wasn't particularly handy with tools, but I did my research and ordered supplies online from Home Depot. When the delivery truck arrived, they laid down two pallets in the driveway and loaded them with 200 concrete pavers, 50 pounds of gravel, 80 pounds of concrete sand, and a container of polymeric sand.

The driver handed me a roll of plastic edging, a rubber mallet, and a hand tamper to level the gravel. I handed him a twenty-dollar bill for his troubles.

What have I gotten myself into? I have no idea what to do with all this stuff.

That was the beginning of a grand adventure into home improvement. After two weeks of digging out a path, laying down gravel, tamping it down to level, and fitting pavers to the curved walkway, I was ready to add the final layer of polymeric sand to hold my mosaic masterpiece together.

I could hardly believe the results. I created something beautiful out of an ugly patch of cement, and nothing could stop me. Next, I extended the sidewalk in the other direction to connect to the back gate. Looking with new eyes at a barren patch of dirt on the other side of the yard, I envisioned a rectangular outdoor dining patio.

That more ambitious project required some outside muscle to dig out the ten-by-twelve-foot rectangle and lug the 24-inch, 35-pound pavers from the driveway. My helpers weren't as meticulous with the level as I was, and the results were less than perfect. But it dramatically transformed our backyard from a desolate wilderness to an idyllic sanctuary.

Like most home improvement projects, the backyard is still a work in progress. Over the years, my partner and I added a pergola, bubbling fountain, mood lighting, and dozens of landscaping plants. But every time we have a barbecue or sit out in the afternoon sun, I marvel at having a hand in creating such beautiful surroundings.

What am I going to do next? It's getting cold, and the pandemic doesn't seem to be leaving. This will be a long winter with nowhere to go and nothing to do.

My home improvement project opened my eyes to the many forms of creativity. I started seeing possibilities everywhere. *I can pull out the batik fabrics I lugged through two moves and make a quilt. I can learn to play the hand drum sitting in its case from last Christmas. I can create an online photo album to share family photos with the next generation.*

It slowly dawned on me that I was creative all along. I just hadn't claimed it. I sewed most of my clothes in junior high school. I wrote and performed plays with the neighborhood kids on the front porch of my parent's barn. I created leaf people from the fallen oak leaves in our backyard and turned oatmeal boxes into Santa Claus containers for homemade cookies.

Why did I give up my college dreams of becoming a dancer or writer? I guess I believed the story that I wasn't one of the gifted ones. Is it too late to create a new story for my third chapter of life?

A few years ago, at an entrepreneurial retreat, I was fascinated by a spiritual writing exercise led by best-selling author and writing coach Tom Bird. After a short meditation with sacred music to connect us to our inner guides, he told us to start writing.

"Don't think about the words," he said. "Just keep your pen on the paper and write whatever words flow through you." The twenty minutes he gave us to capture our soul's desire flew by.

Now I understand what Wayne Dyer said at the Hay House "You Can Change Your Life" conference. The words I'm writing aren't coming from me but flowing through me. I am being divinely led.

Inspired, I enrolled in Bird's "Write a Book in a Weekend" virtual retreat during spring break. Holed up in a scenic hotel on the Chesapeake Bay, surrounded by stunning vistas and blessed silence, we did 30-minute writing stints for three days, broken up with ten-minute stretch breaks and two longer meal breaks. Each session started with a short meditation to get us into the zone, followed by automatic writing without moving our pens from the paper.

My back ached, my fingers cramped, and my restless mind begged for diversions. *Why am I sitting in this air-conditioned hotel room when it's so beautiful outside? Maybe I should take a walk. It must be almost time for a break. Why didn't I bring more snacks? All this thinking is exhausting. I need a nap.* But I stuck with the plan, determined to make the most of this rare opportunity to write something more creative than a law review article.

By the end of the weekend, I filled a large notebook with fragments of my stream-of-consciousness writing. On the last day, we took out a large poster board and tried to organize our thoughts, using Post-it notes to map out our book's beginning, middle, and end.

On the two-hour drive home, my mind was filled with visions of finally becoming a published author. But the same old doubts took over when I reached home.

I have no idea what to do with this mess. There are a lot of words and ideas here, but how am I supposed to turn them into a book? Who cares about my boring life? I don't have anything original to say.

So the poster board full of words and ideas went behind the bookshelf in my home office, where it languished until I retired and had time on my hands.

Maybe I should pull that storyboard out of its hiding place. I don't remember what I was writing about, but I have plenty of time to figure it out.

By some miracle, the storyboard survived the move to North Carolina. The color-coded Post-it notes were faded, and the glue dried up, but they were mostly organized by topic. The notebook pages were intact, and most of the free writing was legible. But I couldn't remember what I thought when I wrote them or what message I intended to convey.

Guess I'll have to go back to the drawing board. At least I'm not starting from scratch. Maybe I'll start by typing the fragments into Microsoft Word. That way, I can cut, paste, and rearrange them until I figure out how they fit together.

That was the origin of my first book, *Shero's Journey*. I was finally a published author, almost 50 years after giving up my childhood dream. Sending a book out into the world gave me the courage to reclaim my creativity, which has flourished ever since. I've written five chapters for collaborative books, dozens of articles on Medium and Substack, and hundreds of blogs and social media posts. Now, I'm working on a dual-timeline historical novel based loosely on my experiences during the 1970s.

The most amazing thing is how it spilled over into other areas of life. I stood up to Ms. Bean's internalized voice and took a drawing course, painted a mandala stone, and took up doodling. I pulled out my mother's best china and set a beautiful table for Thanksgiving. I took a hand-pan lesson and started dancing with my former Nia teacher.

If you think that kind of creativity isn't for you, let me assure you, it is. It's all a matter of perspective. You don't have to be a famous writer, visual artist, musician, or dancer. Once you start viewing the world through a creative lens, you'll begin to see how you've expressed creativity in your daily life without recognizing it.

The next section will introduce you to ten creative archetypes that go beyond the usual stereotypes of visual artists, musicians, authors, or dancers. I guarantee you'll see yourself reflected in one or more of them.

THE PRACTICE

STEP 1: IDENTIFY YOUR CREATIVE ARCHETYPES

We're all familiar with archetypes, even if we don't know the technical definition. Storytellers like Joseph Campbell use them to depict characters on a mythical hero's journey. If I asked you who the hero of Star Wars was, you'd immediately think of Luke Skywalker. If I mentioned the mentor archetype in Harry Potter, Dumbledore would come to mind. That is the power of archetypes. They're part of our collective consciousness and universally recognizable.

The creative archetypes I describe here aren't based on any scientific framework, though they draw on my fascination with the works of Carl Jung, Joseph Campbell, and Carolynn Myss. These archetypes are based on my observations of how people in my personal sphere express their creativity. I think you'll recognize them and probably could develop more creative archetypes from your life experience.

The first step in this tool is to identify which of the creative archetypes sounds most like you. Use your intuition as your guide. Your creative skills may be in the kitchen, garden, or home. They may be connected with other people, animals, or Spirit. You probably never considered them creative, but they're the language you use to express your unique personality and gifts.

As you read the descriptions, highlight or circle words or phrases that resonate with you. We will use them later to develop your creativity roadmap.

THE TRENDSETTER

The trendsetter is talented at spotting what is fresh and new. They know the best shows streaming on Netflix and Hulu and can give you a review of every new restaurant in town. Trendsetters don't only follow the trends. They use their influence to set them. They can throw together an outfit from the thrift store and look like they stepped out of the pages of Vogue magazine. Next thing you know, we're all wearing kilts with lace-up army boots. That's a trendsetter!

THE NATURALIST

The naturalist expresses herself by living in harmony with nature. Naturalists use their creativity to build beautiful gardens, rescue sea turtles, or nurture baby bluebirds in their miniature houses. Their Facebook feeds are filled with photos of ancient trees, blossoming flowers, and intricate spider webs. They create beauty from nature's bounty and live in harmony with their surroundings.

THE DESIGNER

The designer uses her creativity to turn her home into a work of art. Designers follow the latest decorating trends and scour local furniture shops for unique finds. Their homes could be featured in *Architectural Digest*. Designers put thought and creativity into everything they do around the home. Their tables are set with the finest china and crystal, adorned by flowers and candles. Designers turn ordinary moments into extraordinary opportunities to express their creative flair.

THE MAGICIAN

The magician's special genius is the art of creating transformation with a little abracadabra. They love to up-cycle used furniture and vintage clothing from flea markets. Magicians use their resourcefulness to create a silk purse from a sow's ear. They see possibilities everywhere they look and use their creativity to repurpose the old into the new.

THE CRAFTER

The crafter's joy comes from making things with their hands. They love to shop at stores like Michael's or Hobby Lobby for inspiration and enjoy taking up new hobbies like knitting, stained glass, quilting, or woodworking. Crafters enjoy the Zen of keeping their hands busy while socializing or watching television. Crafting makes creativity accessible even to those who didn't excel in art. They get to express their individuality and see something beautiful emerge from nothing.

THE HUMAN CONNECTOR

The human connector has a flair for bringing people together. They put their creativity into throwing the best dinner parties and cultivating friendships with people who bring different interests and perspectives to the table. Human connectors go all out for holidays like Halloween, creating elaborate costumes, decorations, and party games. They love to create a spectacle, and people stand in line to get invited to their parties.

THE SPIRITUAL SEEKER

The spiritual seeker's genius is connecting with a higher power. They use their intuition and vision to interpret Tarot cards, decipher dreams and visions, and bend energy for emotional and physical healing. Spiritual seekers speak in symbols and metaphors. Their genius is in distilling messages from the unknown into language and meaning.

THE CREATIVE GOURMET

Food is the love language of the creative gourmet. They can transform ordinary ingredients into a visually appealing smorgasbord of treats. Creative gourmets love experimenting with different combinations of flavors, tweaking recipes to accentuate their unique take on a favorite dish. Their creativity turns food into a gourmet feast for the eyes and the palate.

THE TRADITIONAL CREATIVE

The traditional creative expresses herself through literature, music, dance, theater, painting, or other visual arts forms. You don't have to be a renowned expert to be a traditional creative. Many of us dabble in the arts, performing in community theater or chorales, writing books or screenplays, or creating visual art for local galleries and art fairs. The problem is we don't think we're good enough to call ourselves creative. Our inner critic sabotages our unique voice, so it's afraid to come out of hiding. To live a more creative life, we may have to give up our dreams of being the next virtuoso and embrace the process of expressing ourselves more freely.

STEP 2: CLAIM YOUR CREATIVE GIFTS

I hope you resonated with one or more of the creative archetypes or created one of your own. Now it's time to claim your gifts and create a plan to amplify their presence in your life.

In this part of the process, you'll follow the clues to your creative expression. Do you always get compliments about something you do but dismiss them because it comes so easily to you? Is there something you love doing so much that you gladly do it for free? Do you have a secret dream of doing something, but your inner critic tells you you're not good enough?

If any of these responses occur to you, it's a hint that you're hiding from your creative genius. Give yourself permission to claim it and see how your creativity expands.

Here are some simple journal prompts to get you thinking.

1. List three ways you already express creativity in your life.
2. List three creative things people always compliment you on.
3. List three creative dreams you have given up.
4. List three things you love so much you would do them every day for free.

STEP 3: DEVELOP YOUR CREATIVE ROAD MAP

The last part of the process seems simple, but it's the most profound. From the lists you created in Step 2, choose three simple steps you could take today to embrace your creativity.

You don't have to start big. When I cleaned out my mother's pantry after she passed away, tucked up on the top shelf, I found an etched, cut glass serving bowl she received as a wedding gift in 1951. Mom often talked about the bowl and imagined bringing it out of hiding for a special occasion. But the special occasion never happened, and the bowl sat in its original box for seventy years.

Mom's bowl, filled with Murano glass fruit, sits on my dining room table as a daily reminder not to wait for a rainy day but to embrace beauty and creativity every moment. Now it's your turn. Identify three simple steps you can take to express your gifts and watch your creativity unfold.

Need some help discovering your creative genius?

Join me for a free call to *Liberate Your Creativity*.

https://calendly.com/lauriemorincoaching/liberate-your-creativity

Laurie Morin is a best-selling author and story doula, helping people birth their life stories into being. Have you always wanted to write a book and have a thousand ideas but don't know where to start? Laurie's gift is helping you parse through the tapestry of your life to identify the story calling you to be told right now.

Laurie's first book, Shero's Journey, is about her journey to live authentically by giving up people-pleasing. It includes writing prompts and deep questions to help you unearth the challenges standing in the way of your dreams and vision.

She is working on her second book, Chasing the 1970s, a dual timeline fictionalized memoir about the parallels between the 1970s and 2020's political and cultural landscapes.

Laurie believes everyone has a story worth telling. Her Jumpstart Your Memoir program provides a roadmap for beginning writers, and her Writer's Circle provides ongoing support for people committed to writing a book. She also leads Culture and Creativity retreats for people ready to nurture their creativity in a sacred setting.

Laurie lives in Wilmington, North Carolina, with her spouse and two spoiled senior dogs, Blondie and Buddy. When not writing, she likes to walk on the beach, garden, and travel to cultural and sacred destinations. She has a white belt in Nia and is studying the ancient art of Qigong.

Let's connect!

Website: https://www.lauriemorin.com

Facebook: https://www.facebook.com/laurie.a.morin

LinkedIn: https://www.linkedin.com/in/authorlauriemorin/

CHAPTER 3

Your Word of the Year

HOW TO CURATE THE LIFE OF YOUR DREAMS

Janette Stuart

MY STORY

My favorite and most powerful tool for transformation is selecting a word of the year. It has allowed me to go from a life of stress and trying to have all the answers to living joyfully each day.

I used to start my day by marching out to my driveway to retrieve the newspaper. I flipped on the morning news before having my first sip of coffee. I scoured the newspaper and watched the news obsessively in case someone asked me a question; I took great pride in knowing the answer, especially about local events.

What if someone asks me about a local project or event I should be aware of, and I don't know the answer?

I don't want to look silly, stupid, or uninformed!

I put a lot of needless pressure on myself.

By using my word of the year, I've gone from needing to know everything to surrendering to divine guidance. This practice helped me curate the life of my dreams by guiding me to live in alignment with my core values.

I employ this simple yet powerful transformation tool many times a day, all year long. Instead of anguishing over what's happening around me or running what-if scenarios, I intentionally focus on what I desire. This shift is enormous. It serves as a focal point, a guidepost, and a theme to guide my decisions and choices.

I often ask myself:

How do I want to feel?

Does this choice align with my word of the year?

If it doesn't align, how can I make a better-feeling decision?

I've embraced the word-of-the-year practice daily for nine years, and it's one of my favorite, most used tools. I credit my dear friend Becky for sharing this potent practice with me. She has been selecting her words of the year for over fourteen years.

When she first mentioned she selected a word of the year, I was puzzled. I didn't grasp its significance or why I might want to adopt the habit myself.

Curious, I asked how she integrated her word of the year into her daily life. She eagerly shared her go-to method: creating a vision board centered around her chosen word.

She revealed a stunning vision board celebrating her word of the year. The images on the board vividly depicted the sensations and experiences she aimed to embrace and cultivate throughout the year. I was mesmerized. The vision board wasn't just a collection of pretty pictures; it was a tangible representation of her aspirations.

As I looked at her vision board, I could see the intentionality behind every image. Each picture resonated with the emotions, dreams, and desires she wanted to manifest. The board wasn't just a passive display—it was an active tool in her daily life. She explained how she gazed at it regularly, allowing its images to reinforce her focus and inspire her actions.

Her practice inspired me to select a word of the year, too, because I could see the tangible results of her happier, more focused, and empowered life.

Who wouldn't want that?

It was like the proverbial "I'll have what she's having" moment as in the movie *When Harry Met Sally*.

As we discussed her practice, I told Becky, "I'm choosing joy as my word of the year for 2016, and we'll see how it works out!" I was so excited.

The word *joy* was a vast departure from how I lived before. I always had a sunny disposition but focused on being a responsible adult, living up to others' expectations, wishes, and desires, which tended to put my joy on the back burner.

Intentionally allowing myself to focus on joy all year was empowering and transformative, and it gave me a childlike zest for life I'd long abandoned.

Later that year, we enjoyed a few days off at the beach. We walked barefoot along the shore, dashing the incoming waves, laughing, and counting our blessings. Becky found a stick that'd washed up in the surf and wrote our words of the year in the wet sand. It was a beautiful moment, seeing our words of the year as a tribute to ourselves and our practice.

Our joy was palpable, a serene culmination of our journey together. The sound of the waves crashing against the shore echoed our laughter, creating a symphony of nature and delight that we would cherish forever.

I wholeheartedly embraced joy that year and steeped myself in its incredible energy, which made me feel lighter, happier, more energetic, and more carefree. My joy was a beacon. It was a contagion for good, and it hooked me for life on selecting a word of the year.

Speaking of joy, my favorite quote about joy is:

"You are joy, looking for a way to express.
It's not just that your purpose is joy; it is that you are joy.
You are love and joy and freedom and clarity expressing.
Energy - frolicking and eager - that's who you are.
And so, if you're always reaching for alignment with that,
you're always on your path, and your path will take you
into all kinds of places."

~ Abraham-Hicks

I begin my day in stillness with a few moments of devotion and ponder how I'll use my word of the year. I intentionally focus on how I want to feel during my day. It's a huge departure from my days of relentlessly following current events. I no longer even watch the news—such a huge relief.

Does this mean there are never moments of doubt, difficulties, or wrong turns along the way? No, not at all. After all, I'm human, and mistakes, bumps in the road, and unplanned twists and turns are part of the journey.

When I stray from my desired intention and find myself off-kilter, off-balance, or misaligned, I can begin again by lovingly giving myself the grace to reset and make a better-feeling choice.

Here's a list of the empowering words I've chosen as my words of the year over the last nine years.

- Joy
- Delight
- Trust
- Flourish
- Celebrate
- Miracles
- Wonder
- Gratitude
- Reverence

Imagine how focusing on these words, or words like them, could've altered your life over the past nine years.

Of course, these are my words of the year; yours will be equally unique and meaningful. I'll show you how to select your word of the year in the practice section below. Your word must resonate with you, as you'll use it as a guidepost or focal point to manifest the life of your dreams.

Delight was my word of choice for 2017, and I sure did have a delightful year. It was a year of deep creativity where I self-published two books and created my first inspirational card deck called "Love Notes from The Divine." Truly a delight.

While pondering my word for 2018, the energy felt different. *Trust* kept bubbling up, but it wasn't as juicy or lighthearted as joy or delight had been. I was initially resistant to choosing the word trust, but I leaned into the guidance I received and selected it.

The angels guided me to create a trust manifesto and whispered *trust the best is yet to come*. This guidance about trust was a blessing to receive because, at the time, I was in my late fifties, a time when others might think their best years were behind them. You can read about both on my blog.

Late in 2018, I felt unwell and thought I was doing too much and pushing myself too hard. I trusted that better days were ahead even when I had zero energy, had trouble eating, and lost 30 pounds without trying.

Four days into 2019, I was diagnosed with pancreatic cancer, and my word of the year was *flourish*. This word was one of the most powerful and healing words of the year for me to choose. Many times a day, I asked myself: *How can I flourish now?*

Flourishing took many forms. Sometimes, it meant enjoying a nap, taking an anti-nausea pill, brewing a soothing cup of tea, or reaching out to a friend or loved one.

I did flourish despite the scary diagnosis, dismal survival rate, chemotherapy, losing my hair, and having an extensive life-saving surgery.

In 2020, I chose the word *celebrate*. I survived my healing journey with pancreatic cancer and looked for ways I could celebrate my vibrant health. I also had my diamond jubilee birthday that year. I decided to celebrate by writing sixty hand-written letters to friends and family who helped me and my family along the way. I also bought postage stamps with the word *celebrate* to amp up the experience.

I bought a necklace with the hand-hammered word *celebrate* inscribed on it, and it included a terracotta bead for essential oil, which I wore daily. I couldn't resist the *celebration* oil blend to anoint myself daily.

I was also blessed to contribute a chapter called *Gratitude: The Magic Elixir to Reduce Stress, Worry, and Anxiety* in the #1 bestseller *The Wellness Universe Guide to Complete Self-Care* by Anna Pereira and published by Brave Healer Productions.

In 2021, I was on the lookout for *miracles* daily. I listed miracles, big or small, on a small piece of paper and placed them in a pretty glass jar I kept on my dining room table. Sometimes, I shared the miracles I discovered with loved ones or treasured friends. At the end of the year, I had a ceremony and read my miracles, which was a fantastic way to close out the year.

In 2022, my focus was *wonder*. I often found wonder during my daily walks in nature or at my hummingbird feeder, and I frequently shared wonder pictures on social media.

In 2023, *gratitude* was my daily focus. I have a private Facebook group called Angel Circle of Gratitude and host a 30-day gratitude journey each November. Part of my gratitude practice was writing thirty postcards to folks who have inspired me over the years. I also created a 30-day gratitude journey booklet as an opt-in with favorite quotes about gratitude, affirmation cards, and journaling pages, which includes my chapter on gratitude, mentioned three paragraphs above.

My word of the year for 2024 is *reverence*. I created a vision board about how reverence feels and gaze at it daily. I chose a lovely, hard-cover, gold-leaf quality journal with gorgeous artwork that depicted reverence to me from my favorite vendor, Peter Pauper Press. It has a full moon shining over a woodland setting, illuminating colorful flowers on the front and back covers. It feels magical and sacred, evoking a true sense of reverence for me. I often record where or how I've experienced reverence or add quotes that spark awe within this beautiful space.

By selecting a word of the year, I focus on what I want more of in my life instead of worrying about what's wrong, falling into a rabbit hole of anxiety, or trying to know it all.

As you can see by the many examples above, I've embraced my words of the year and found countless ways to embody and express them over the years. Be creative; do what lights you up.

Motivational speaker Tony Robbins shares that where focus goes, energy flows. And where energy flows, whatever you're focusing on grows. In other words, your life is controlled by what you focus on.

What are you focusing on? Is it empowering you or zapping your life-force energy? What do you want more of in your life?

So, what do you want to curate, dear reader? A life of your dreams or more of the same thing every day? It's up to you.

THE PRACTICE

SELECTING YOUR WORD OF THE YEAR EXERCISE

What you'll need:

• Journal or paper

• Favorite writing instrument

• Water, or favorite drink

Get comfortable so you can write with ease.

Give yourself the gift of solitude for at least 30 minutes.

On the top of your paper, draw the outlines of a heart and a cloud, side by side. You'll want these images big enough to hold five or six words.

Leave the heart and cloud images alone for the time being. You'll begin listing words below them.

Have you thought of a word of the year that you might select? If so, write that word down below the heart and cloud shapes. If you don't have any words coming to mind, that's fine.

Take a deep breath and get comfortable. Everything you do during this process will be easy and fun. You can't get it wrong.

Don't force anything; allow yourself to receive with an open heart and mind. Don't overthink or stress about any of this exercise. It's okay if your paper is messy; it's just for you.

Let's do a visualization. Close your eyes and place your hand on your heart. Please take a deep breath and let it out.

Imagine feeling cozy, protected, and safe in a favorite spot. The temperature is just perfect for you, and you feel serene.

Let yourself look forward to next year at this time. If at any time during this visualization, you think of a word or words that call to you, write them down on your paper. Don't try to remember them as you go along. You'll have quite a list of words to choose from. Whatever words or feelings come to you are perfect.

Ponder these questions and write the answers on your paper.

- How do I want to feel during the year ahead?
- What areas of my life am I hoping to strengthen or enhance?
- Think about your favorite colors. How do they make you feel when you wear or see them?

Read the following list of words; write them down on your paper if they energize or delight you. If another word comes to mind, write it down also.

Joy	Delight	Trust	Flourish
Celebrate	Wonder	Reverence	
Miracles	Gratitude		

Here's another list of words that may interest you. Read the list; if anything sparks you, write them down on your paper.

Abundance	Healthy	Opportunities	Vibrant
Beauty	Independence	Possibilities	Wellbeing
Creativity	Joy	Quiet	Excitement
Devotion	Kindness	Renewal	Yes
Empowered	Lightness	Stillness	Zest
Freedom	Mindfulness	Tenderness	
Grateful	Nourish	Unique	

During this final part of the visualization, write down the letters of the alphabet on the left-hand side of your paper, leaving enough room next to each letter to add a word or words that energize, uplift, or inspire you.

Write this list as quickly as possible. If a word doesn't materialize for a letter, skip it and proceed to the following letter. Allow it to be fun and easy.

Now that you have many words on your paper, review them, pick your favorite five, and circle them.

Write those five circled words inside the heart image at the top of your page.

Look at those five words inside the heart image. What do those words have in common? They may bring another sensation or word to you. If so, add that word inside the heart.

Next, circle your three favorite words from inside your heart image. What do those words have in common? Is there one you are reacting to the most? Which one energizes and uplifts you the most? Write that word in the cloud image if one is singing to you.

If you love the word in the cloud image, congratulations, you've just created your focus word of the year.

If you need help with the process, please email janette@angel-angles.com and let me know. I've guided hundreds of people in successfully selecting their words of the year.

Here's an invitation to join us in our cozy community to develop your word of the year for 2025 on Zoom on December 27, 2024. Join free and register now: https://bit.ly/CreateWordfor2025

Janette Stuart is a beacon of hope and joy that shines brightly in a world often clouded by uncertainty and challenges. As the Emissary of Joy at Angel Angles and Well-Being and Wonder, she's a best-selling author, angelic practitioner, and triumphant pancreatic cancer survivor.

Through the thousands of angel card readings she has conducted, her gentle approach helps clients find clarity, direction, and divine guidance.

As the Angelic Practitioner Expert Guide at The Wellness Universe for several years, her monthly angel affirmations are among their most popular blogs.

Her courses, books, card decks, and events are gateways to peace, inspiration, and transformation, empowering you to stand and shine as only you can.

Janette knew she'd be an author at age eight. She credits this to a great Christmas gift: a feathered pen and a locking diary. There, she shared her feelings, dreams, and desires within that sacred space. She has self-published five books and participated in nine amazing collaborations.

Janette is a fourth-generation Californian who lives with her husband of 41 years in the Bay Area. Their love story includes eloping during a blizzard on a Greyhound bus, a grown son, and two grandchildren.

She's passionate about self-care because she used to put herself last for far too long, which left her depleted, resentful, and sick.

Get your gift: Self-Care Strategies, a 37-page booklet delivered to your inbox to enhance or begin your self-care practice. It's full of great tips, tools, and techniques. Visit https://bit.ly/SelfCareStrategies4U

Connect with Janette Stuart:

Website: https://www.angel-angles.com

Email: janette@angel-angles.com

Instagram: https://www.instagram.com/angel_angles_101/

Facebook: https://www.facebook.com/AngelAngles11

CHAPTER 4

Finding Yourself After Trauma

UNDERSTANDING YOUR EXPERIENCES EMBRACING THEIR GIFTS

Sara Jane

"As traumatized children, we always dreamed someone would come and save us. We never dreamed it would, in fact, be ourselves as adults."

~ Alice Little

We should never judge what can be traumatic to a child; a single word, a tone of voice, or an action can bring their world tumbling down around them.

Children aren't as resilient as adults seem to think; they don't understand or know how to deal with mental and emotional pain. So much so that they bury their feelings deep within them. They may have no memory of what happened or how they felt, but it all still lies at a deep cellular memory level.

MY STORY

It's early 1959. Baby Jane was sitting on the kitchen floor curiously watching her mother. *What is she doing?*

There was a table with a cloth on it; her mother was making a cup of coffee with boiling milk, put it on the table, and stepped away.

Shuffling across the floor, Jane pulled the edge of the cloth. There was a splash, a scream, and a crash as the cup of coffee went over her face, down her neck, and seeped into the jumper she wore.

Having had nursing training, her mother grabbed her and ran her under the cold tap before running across the road to the doctor's surgery for an ambulance to be called.

In the late 1950s, most homes didn't have phones, and even fewer had two cars.

The jumper Jane was wearing stuck to her skin, and she wouldn't leave the resulting wounds alone. Jane was in the hospital for three months and "crucified," the term used by the hospital for pinning her arms so she couldn't scratch the affected area.

The hospital's rules were that her parents could only visit her for an hour every other day. However, due to the distance they lived from the hospital, they could only see her once a week for an hour.

Why don't mummy and daddy come to see me? What have I done wrong? Don't they love me anymore?

There were so many tears and feelings she couldn't understand or name, running rife through her tiny being—confusion, feeling lost, and so very unhappy. All she wanted was to be hugged and cuddled, to feel loved and cared for, and for the pain and hurt to go away.

It didn't matter how many loving, soothing, calming words her mother spoke to her; she still left without taking Jane with her.

As the weeks rolled on, she calmed, resigning herself to these strange feelings.

Then one day her parents came and took her home, only this wasn't a home she recognized, it was strange and unfamiliar, except for one thing. *My teddy bear, a familiar friend at last.*

Life ticked on, and in August, her sister Gillian was born, sadly an unwell baby who spent time in and out of hospital.

When she was nine weeks old, Gillian died in her sleep at home in her cot.

As her mother was packing Gillian's things in a cupboard, Jane asked, "Baby in cupboard?"

Jane was only 18 months old and loved unconditionally—first her parents and then Gillian. She was gone. *I've been left again; no one loves me.*

Yes, this is my story, the start of it; I was less than a year old and spent my first birthday in hospital. I have no memories of what happened, only what I've been told over the years and an educated guess as to how this precious little girl must have felt.

In the years that followed, other things compounded my feelings of insecurity, setting the scene for the next 30-plus years. Thank goodness for my teddy bear; *he never let me down.*

I was painfully shy, becoming a people-pleaser. I always said yes and constantly tried to figure out what others would like so they would be happy and with the hope they'd like me. Even if it was only for a short while until they realized I wasn't worth liking or loving.

I went into automatic mode; I existed, doing what had to be done, saying what I thought I should say, and behaving in ways that hopefully kept other people happy. So much of it is a blur; there are so few memories for me to look back on.

Why would I wish to remember a time in my life when I was so unhappy? I felt unwanted, unloved, not good enough, and unworthy for years. The rejection and abandonment of my first year left me both mentally and emotionally scared. I didn't understand and didn't know how to deal with the feelings I couldn't even put a name to.

Somewhere in there, when my parents moved to a new town, I changed my name from Jane to Sara, which is why I started my story the way I did.

Without realizing it, I created self-fulfilling prophecies in my life that relationships wouldn't last and anything (including jobs and marriages) would end.

As important as my early life is to my story, after all, I wouldn't be who I am today and doing what I do without it. The wake-up call brought light-bulb moments that helped me find myself.

It's December 1996. I'm living in Northampton with my second husband, Kevin. *I hate going to the dentist, and yet here I am, having to have a wisdom tooth out because of an abscess.* Very ironic considering what happened next.

The numbing injections, three of them, weren't fully working; I felt the dentist pulling and tugging on the tooth. I clenched my hands around the arms of the chair, grunting in pain. *Crack!* Then another. "Don't worry, that is normal," I was told. It didn't give up easily.

It's finally out. Now I can relax. Kevin took me home.

I was in the bedroom when the pain started. *Why is it hurting so much? So much pain!* I was on my knees and put my face against the hot radiator, tears rolling down my cheeks.

It got worse over the next few days. *Something isn't right. I can barely open my mouth, I am struggling with chewing, and I can't get my toothbrush between my teeth to clean them. Did my jaw move in a way it shouldn't?*

A week later, Kevin took me to the hospital.

A very disbelieving triage nurse told me, "Dentists don't break jaws; you will have to wait, and it could be up to four hours."

Me: "I'll wait."

The doctor who saw me sent me for an X-ray.

"Please clamp your teeth around the mouthpiece and remain still."

"I can't open my mouth wide enough to do that."

"Do the best you can."

While I waited for the results, the triage nurse came in. I don't remember the words she used, but now she believed me; my jaw was broken.

At long last, someone listened and believed me.

I was sent home for the night and asked to come back the following day for my jaw to be operated on.

Back at the hospital, the operation took two hours as they tried to put my jaw back into place and insert pins to secure it.

When I came around, the nurse said, "You became violent."

It was only later that I realized there must have been a lot of pain. For many years, I was affected by period pains and lay in bed kicking my legs; I'm guessing I did the same as the aesthetic wore off.

Or could this have harked back to when I was in pain at the age of one and the stored trauma in my body?

My husband picked me up the next day, took me home, and warmed up some of my homemade soup for me. The following day, it became clear, purely by his attitude, that the caring stopped, and I was expected to continue as if nothing happened.

Six months of pain and sleepless nights followed with numerous painkillers and sleeping tablets that didn't work.

I was exhausted, but eventually, morphine broke the cycle of pain and spasms.

At the same time, I worked full time, studied for accountancy exams, ran a home, and still managed full-time people pleasing.

Something has to give.

I stopped attending my course and started learning a little about homeopathy, including the benefits of arnica and ignatia to support me through the shock and trauma, not just of the broken jaw, but as it turned out, my childhood trauma as well.

Then in October 1997, I broke up my marriage. We were together for 11 years but only married for three and a half.

I temporarily moved into the spare bedroom before moving into a rented house. At the same time, work told us the company was being taken over, and we could either go to the new company in Bournemouth or take severance pay.

Somehow, I saw this as a new beginning and a gift. In August 1998, I started my move to Bournemouth. I stayed with the company for the transition period, to support the transfer of information from our systems to theirs. I bought my little house in February 1999 and took redundancy in April, walking straight into a new job within six days over the Easter period.

Now I am free to discover who I am. I asked to see a psychotherapist to help me understand why I'd been the way I'd been, and it helped me to gain an insight into my story and the circumstances that contributed to it.

I always knew what happened and the circumstances surrounding it. The awareness that not everything is in our control came much later, along with the understanding that my parents were affected by the rules of the hospital.

I wasn't abandoned or rejected; it was circumstances. Sadly, however, that isn't how it felt to a one-year-old.

A recent thought: *Is it the incident that causes the trauma or the feelings it activates in us? Especially if we felt we weren't listened to or believed, felt ignored, rejected, abandoned, filling us full of feelings of being unloved, unwanted, or not good enough.*

It isn't necessarily the physicality of what happened that causes us the greatest pain.

Especially if we have become people-pleasers and, I can speak from experience: we lose ourselves and who we are. We become who others tell us to be to keep them happy, and sadly, we can become all too easily controlled.

But it doesn't have to be this way. Are you ready to learn to say no to others and give yourself permission to find out who you are? Are you ready to let go of everything others have told you to be and explore yourself and the world, having new experiences regardless of what others may say?

I did this. In February 2000, I joined a group from the Scientific Exploration Society, which traveled to Romania to work with the Carpathian Large Carnivore Project tracking wolves and lynx in the Carpathian Mountains. We were there for two weeks. Nobody knew me; I could be me.

Before that, in 1999, I abseiled off the water tower in Poole to help raise money for a charity; in the old days, my mother's reaction would've stopped me.

Over the next 20 years, I experienced many different things. I took myself to Egypt to see dolphins in the wild and, in 2005, took a small group of adults with learning difficulties to America, a project I called Spirit of Freedom, to spend time with the Nez Perce in Idaho. We also visited Yellowstone National Park.

THE PRACTICE

UNEARTHING YOUR TRUE SELF

Do you know who you are?

Would you like to discover the *you* buried beneath all you've been told you are by others?

The suggestions and thoughts I share here have all supported me in finding myself and being true to who I am. They're suggestions—because it's important to find what works for you and speaks to you to support you on your healing journey. Go at your own pace.

1. Learn as much as you can about the circumstances of your early life, the highs and lows, and the challenges and experiences. Reflect on the information, especially the lows, to come to understand them; you don't have to like them.

Ask about the experiences your parents and grandparents went through growing up, listen to their stories. Many indigenous peoples (Native Americans, the Aborigines, the Māori) all share their wisdom and history through storytelling.

What we witness within our family home shapes us. In many cases, it forms how and who we become.

Doing this can support the adult you with an understanding your younger you didn't have, helping and supporting you when connecting with your younger self.

2. Your first name, given name, is very important and powerful, especially the name your mother called you as a young child.

Start by speaking your name out loud to yourself, and repeat it over and over, gently and calmly. You're asking nothing of yourself, only acknowledging yourself, the whole of who you are. Feel its resonance.

By giving yourself the space to do this, you can then sit and feel any changes that start to occur within you. Your younger self will start to feel seen, and you can always sit quietly and see if they will communicate with you.

You can also tone your name. Some may call it singing, incorporating the energy of sound into the practice. The best way to do this is to break your name down into syllables. For example, *Sa Ra, Ja Nine, Vir Gi Nia, Da Vid, Scott.*

HOW I CAME TO UNDERSTAND THE IMPORTANCE OF OUR NAME.

I was blessed to live close to some heathland and walked there regularly. I love being out in nature. One day, I was talking to Jane. I can't remember what I was saying when suddenly the thought hit me. *The only person who had ever rejected me was me when I changed my name from Jane to Sara.*

I was christened Sara Jane and now use my whole name to honor the whole of me and who I am.

I understand that far too many of us don't like our names, probably because of the memories of being told off or always being asked to do something or not, but this little exercise can help you change that.

When working with clients I tone their name (the one their mother called them); it has a profound effect.

3. *Why am I worrying about what others think about me when they aren't?*

This thought came to me one day as I stood in the kitchen. It was as if a lightbulb went on and a massive weight lifted off my shoulders.

Especially for you people-pleasers constantly worrying about what others think of you, I hope it helps you in the same way it has me.

> *"What other people think and say about you*
> *is none of your business. The most destructive thing you*
> *would ever do is to believe someone else's opinion of you.*
> *You have to stop letting other people's opinions control you."*
> ~ Wayne Dyer

4. Affirmations. This is an affirmation I use every day (and have for years), along with others. Please feel free to use it or re-word it as it feels comfortable for you.

As I acknowledge and release my past

Old wounds heal at last

Now I live for today

And know it is special in every way

I am special; I love me

My Gift: A Mediation: Meet your younger self.

At the foot of my bio, you will find a link to experience a meditation to meet your younger self.

Suggestion: On the first listening, invite in a happy aspect of yourself, helping them to get to know you and feel comfortable and safe in your company.

When you're ready, do the meditation again, this time inviting in any part of you that wishes to come forward, helping and supporting your inner child (your younger self) to trust you.

I'm sure that once you've done it a couple of times you'll be able to take yourself into the meditation whenever you choose, and the connection, love, and trust with all aspects of you will grow, building your confidence in who you are and your abilities.

Whatever your story, if you would like support, find someone who will listen, someone you feel comfortable with.

Our stories may not be the same but many of us can relate to and empathize with the feelings they caused.

There is a lovely line in a poem called "Be Yourself" by Bruce B Wilmer:

*"Wisdom lies in what you've learned
and what you have withstood."*

Who is **Sara Jane**? She is the sum of all her experiences, including the story shared above.

Prior to 2005, Sara had worked in retail to area manager level, office management for two toy companies, managed public houses with her first husband, went into insurance, and worked with children with learning disabilities and behavioral problems.

In 2005, she took the leap to go self-employed as a complementary health therapist, learning Indian Head Massage, Metamorphic Technique, Thai foot massage, ear candling, and Quantum Touch, along with Reiki and sound in the form of toning, a practice that has grown into Vocal Reiki.

Sara is the creator of Vocal Reiki and has discovered the most powerful gift it brings is to support people to connect with and heal their inner child, the youngest aspects of themselves which were affected by hurt, pain, and trauma.

She is a teacher, holding workshops and courses in person and online, and is an international speaker and author.

Sara is the founder of Gift of Healing TV which she started in 2014. It is a live weekly program sharing interviews with practitioners of many different techniques and practices that support health and well-being on all levels.

They also share mediations, exercises, and conversations to support you on your healing journey. The recordings of all the programs are on the catch-up pages of the website creating a wonderful free resource for you to explore.

Sara has discovered she is a channel for dragons and many other mythical beings. As well as sharing monthly messages from them, she channels messages in Light Language.

Connect with Sara:

Vocal Reiki: https://vocalreiki.com/

Gift of Healing TV: https://www.giftofhealingtv.com/

Our Mythical Friends: https://ourmagicalfriends.com/

Facebook: https://www.facebook.com/SaraJane.SpiritOfFreedom

LinkedIn: https://www.linkedin.com/in/sara-jane-94b9a117/

Free Meditation: https://vocalreiki.com/gifts-of-wisdom-meditation/

CHAPTER 5

Yoga Nidra

AN INTENTION TO RELAX AND EASE THE MIND

Denyse LeFever, MBA, C-IAYT

"The more we can develop a healthy relationship with all parts of life, not just the parts we like or want to experience, the better off we'll be. We need to learn not just how to feel good, but also to get comfortable with feeling bad."

~ Kamini Desai[1]

MY STORY

The stomach churn is relentless.

Suppose my college board scores are a disaster. I'll never get into college. I'm not as smart as my classmates.

Palms moist with sweat, tears on the brink of spilling over.

Why am I a complete failure? I'll never amount to anything.

---

1 https://www.kaminidesai.com/single-post/from-toxic-positivity-to-pure-life

My 16-year-old head chatter was overwhelming—crippling at times. Fortunately, my astute mother intervened. After listening to my worries, she said.

"You'll have a nervous breakdown if you don't stop fretting. The school offers a beginner's yoga class in the adult evening program. Sign up."

In 1970, the fall of my junior year, I walked into an evening yoga class in the gym. Everyone was older than me. I searched for an unoccupied corner of the room. Slowly, my awkward body moved to instructor-directed stretches, twists, and new shapes. Simple movements felt surprisingly good. I moved with ease. In no time at all, the movement practice was over. We were asked to lie down for relaxation.

The teacher guided us: "Tune into your breath. Imagine you're on a sunny beach."

The hard, polished wooden gym floor transitioned to a soft, powder-white beach. My body relaxed into the sand image.

My breath is deep and calm. Golden sunlight is warming my face. I feel the warmth spread through my whole body. I smell the salt air. I hear waves crashing on the shore. I am relaxed.

The visualization was over in less than ten minutes. My mind chatter was silent.

After one class, the impact on my body sensations was subtle, but the impact on my mental and emotional state was profound. I was hooked. College boards were looming, but my tummy and mind were calm.

I continued with the beginner class and added a yoga philosophy and breath/meditation class. These practices didn't get rid of my adolescent mind chatter, but worry didn't cripple me as often.

My practice was personal and private. None of my friends practiced yoga. Yoga became my secret coping weapon.

Life continued. Uncertainty created mind chatter.

My college board scores aren't great, but I received a college acceptance letter. I don't want to go. I'm not ready for college. I'll flunk out, do drugs, or become an alcoholic.

Tears and worries took over my senior year despite my ongoing yoga and meditation practice.

"Take a gap year," my parents suggested.

I need to test my independence before I experience unsupervised peer pressure in college.

I spent a gap year with family and friends in London and worked as a mother's helper. I breathed and meditated.

My secret yoga practice throughout my twenties continued to ease my mind chatter as I faced life decisions. However, a literature and foreign languages degree didn't help me find work in a competitive job market.

I want to be a writer, but I'll never be able to support myself as a writer. Who will hire a liberal arts graduate and pay me enough so I can live on my own? I want to travel the world and meet interesting people from different cultures, and I don't even speak languages that well.

Yoga kept me balanced as I hopped through minimum-wage jobs every year.

Finally, a family member helped me land a job as a French/English translator/clerk typist at a leading aerospace and defense contractor under contract with the Tunisian government. I swapped English for basic electronic tutoring with about a dozen Tunisian military personnel undergoing technical training at the company.

Noting my rapport with the company's customers, my boss encouraged me, "You should attend business school. We'll cover the tuition."

As I began my MBA, the project ended. I was laid off.

I looked for work, and I continued my part-time MBA studies. My savings were being depleted. I found a job with a small niche aerospace company. The smaller size created a great learning opportunity. I interacted with fascinating international customers. I loved the work, but the work environment was overly demanding.

Mom came to the rescue once again. "I've just learned about a place called Kripalu in Massachusetts. Go there for a yoga retreat. I think you need it."

I started to feel successful at my job, but my rumination continued:

I'm thirty, getting old and fat. Why can't I meet a nice guy and settle into a normal life? No one will ever love me. Guys don't understand my international interests or work schedule. I travel internationally and meet new people, but I'm paid much less than all the men. They seem to find time for vacation. Why can't I get all my work done? I'll be a clerk for the rest of my life. I don't want to end up as a bag lady.

One day, I told my boss, "I'm taking a spa vacation in New England to work on losing weight."

He'll understand a fat farm self-improvement break better than a yoga retreat.

My lifestyle was taking a toll on my waistline.

At Kripalu, I signed up for a workshop called "Inner Quest Intensive." It delivered intense inner work. The silent retreat guided us to connect to our Self through deep meditation. The participants were nothing like my work colleagues. I judged them as touchy-feely hippies who vocally experienced every emotion as they moved and meditated. Based on the noisy, emotional outbursts from the hippie participants, intensive questing happened all around me. I tried to ignore the moans and groans and went deeper into myself.

I thought this was a silent retreat. Ignore them. I don't belong here. I'm not enough. I'm not happy. Why am I here? That guy sounds like he's in real pain. I'm not at all like these people. Will I ever find love? I grew up in a stable, loving family. Why am I so miserable?

On day two, the guided meditation encouraged us to meet our spirit guide and listen to its wisdom. I reserved my judgments about spirit guides and focused on my breath:

My breath is slowing down, getting deeper. An image of a pristine white sandy beach along a Caribbean blue surf appears. As I wade through the surf, my feet are wet but warm. In the distance, I see a lean, attractive woman about my age with short, curly brown hair. The ocean breeze blows softly against her long white dress as it billows in the wind. She splashes through the water's edge and heads toward me. "Hi, I'm Miranda." She greets me. "I want you to know that you are enough. Your discontent is valid, but it's temporary. You will find your way." She touches my chest, and a golden white light floods my being. I feel a charge of healing energy. I'm rejuvenated and entirely at ease.

I emerged from the meditation feeling transformed and lighter. I floated to the evening meal. In my mind, Miranda meant "seeing" from the Spanish verb *mirar*, which translates as "to look at, watch, or pay close attention to." At dinner, others in the class remarked that my face was transformed, serene, and peaceful. I knew there was a profound shift.

I left the retreat vowing to leave my work environment. I took a new job with a Fortune 500 aerospace company. I began to accept that the "right" relationship with another may not happen. I decided to believe Miranda's words.

I am enough. I didn't need anyone else.

My career became my focus. I had no career objective other than to learn and experience as much as possible. Over the next two decades, the company I joined transferred me to four different locations and merged many times. I also met my love. My career and family became my priorities. Miranda and my yoga practices became a distant memory.

My company measured our progress by how well we achieved our annually stated goals. Goal achievement led to increased opportunity and pay. These goals defined our desired position in the company. I resisted stating what I wanted to achieve. My boss insisted I name it—director or vice president. Doubt returned.

I am not qualified for this job. They needed a woman in this management position to meet their quotas. I don't have the technical background to do this work. It's not just my job at stake; now, there's a team counting on me. I'm not a leader. I'm going to let them down.

Ben and Jerry's *Phish Food* or *Chubby Hubby* medicated my state of mind. Physically, I wasn't well. I started exercising. I maintained a similar frantic, cardiac-racing pace in my exercise regimen that I applied to my job.

The pounding on the treadmill took its toll. Foot problems, which were first diagnosed after a racquet ball-induced stress fracture in my thirties, were no longer responding to holistic treatments.

"You need foot surgery on both feet," the doctor told me.

In 2004, I was confined to bed for several weeks as I healed from toe fusion surgery on my right foot. At the same time, another company merger meant more organizational change at my job. I called into daily meetings with my boss from my bedside office to brainstorm the future organization structure. He suggested that I move from my location in New York State to corporate offices in DC. He agreed to wait to make the change until I healed from my foot surgery.

Transitioning from a rural, relatively small business unit to a major metropolitan corporate office was more stressful than anticipated. Now in my 50s, I was excited by the challenge, but the traffic, housing prices, and cost of living overwhelmed me. Shortly after we sold our house in New York and found a new one almost four times the cost in Virginia, my boss told me he was leaving the company. Corporate began to consolidate functions, reorganize, and downsize.

My new colleagues and I speculated about our futures.

I joked. "Each workday is like an episode on the TV show Survivor. Who's going to get voted off the island?"

We started creating plots for a reality TV show to amuse ourselves during persistent organizational rumors.

Driving home from work one evening, I received a call from my doctor. "Your blood work is in. I want to meet you in person tomorrow."

"You have type 2 diabetes." She clinically announced the next day. "We're going to put you on metformin right away, and I want you to focus on losing weight. I'll follow up with you in thirty days."

I was stunned. *This has to be a mistake.*

The following month, my doctor consulted her notes, "You also need blood pressure and cholesterol medications."

I looked at her, and the tears flowed freely.

"What's wrong?"

"I've never been on prescription medications. Is this my life now?" I sobbed.

She sharply responded without empathy. "You should feel thankful that we have drugs to treat this. In the past, people got complications and died."

Her bluntness and guidance not to eat mangos are all I remember from my initial diagnosis.

I studied my condition and managed it as best I could. I knew that in addition to eating healthy foods, exercise was necessary. My foot problems meant changing my treadmill-pounding exercise, so I joined a yoga studio.

After sharing the latest imagined *Survivor* plot with my co-workers, I rushed to the studio during rush hour traffic. I was on edge, a tense spring, getting ready to break. I chuckled to myself:

Something's not right if you are stressed out going to a yoga class.

The yoga style was gentle, but movement and stillness were more difficult than in my 30s. Grief overcame me. We moved into the final relaxation pose. I couldn't relax. My mind raced. My body was tight.

I can't get my body to relax. What happened to me? My movements don't flow. My body used to move smoothly. It's now jerky and tight.

Tears began to leak out.

I'm holding tension everywhere. Where is the ease that I once knew?

I persisted with a weekly practice. My left foot pain was excruciating. I shopped doctors in the area to find one who also worked with type 2 diabetes patients. I knew my age and condition had the potential for complications. I found a well-known doctor who performed my third foot surgery.

At home, after the surgery, the pain medication didn't work.

This is worse than the previous ones. My bones throb. The pain is radiating from my toes up my leg. I'm so tired. I can't sleep. I can't find a comfortable position. I can't look at the metal rods coming out of my toes. I'm sleepy. I hurt. Something is wrong.

My husband empathized with my pain. He asked to remove the bandage and check it out. The second toe was very swollen and had turned a dark blue-black. He called the doctor, who agreed to see me right away.

"Oh, that doesn't look good. What do you think happened?"

What do I think happened? You're the goddamn doctor!

"I think you are going to lose the toenail at best. I'll try to save the toe, but I can't promise anything. You won't be able to play golf or do yoga again."

Miserable, I returned home, lay in bed, and felt sorry for myself.

I'm too young to feel so old. I can live without golf, but not yoga. When was the last time I felt okay?

As I drifted off into a painkiller-induced nap, Miranda appeared. "Now might be a good time to deepen your yoga studies."

I woke up with a hazy memory of meeting Miranda and sent a note to my yoga teacher. "I want to learn more about yoga but do not want to teach." I caveated.

Two months later, I returned to work. A change of CEOs meant another restructuring. In January 2010, I sat in a chair wearing a surgical boot in a yoga studio and began a 300-hour yoga teacher training program. I was the class's oldest, heaviest, tightest woman. I gradually found balance—physically, mentally, emotionally. Six months later, I took an early retirement package from my corporate job. Thanks to Miranda, I continue to live in balance, do yoga, read, learn, relax, and enjoy new experiences with less intense mind chatter.

> *"Within you, there is a stillness and a sanctuary*
> *to which you can retreat at any time and be yourself."*
> ~ Hermann Hesse, Siddhartha

THE PRACTICE

Yoga Nidra, or yogic sleep, is a profound guided meditation technique that connects you to your Self. I AM™ Yoga Nidra, developed by Kamini Desai, Ph.D., is a version of this practice I experienced at Kripalu.

Yoga Nidra invites us to set an intention. For some, an intention may suggest an action-oriented goal. This is not the case. Its purpose is to encourage a positive state of being. The intention may appear in images, words, or a present-tense sentence expressing a quality you wish to experience.

As an example, perhaps you have anxiety or worry. The intention is positive:

I approach my day with peaceful confidence.

Not:

I will not worry. I won't be anxious.

Being peaceful and confident may help you achieve a goal, but it is not necessary to accomplish it.

It can be difficult for someone new to this practice to develop an intention spontaneously. To help get comfortable with intention setting, I've created the following mudra or hand gesture and breath practice. It can be done stand-alone or before Yoga Nidra. If any aspect of this practice makes you feel uneasy, it may be a chance for self-exploration. Or you may pause the practice. Go to https://youtu.be/CpZRKyL_0d0 for a video of this practice.

1. **Dhyana Mudra – Gesture of Meditation:** Find a comfortable seated position. Gently close your eyes. Arrange your hands so the right palm is on the left, facing up. The thumbs are slightly lifted. Tips are touching. Allow the hands to rest on your lap or near your navel. Take a few breaths. Inhale through the nose. Exhale as though blowing out a candle. Repeat five times. Notice what thoughts or images arise. Allow your breath to return to its natural rhythm.

2. **Kapota Mudra – Gesture of the Dove**: Bring your palms together at the heart, but hold them slightly away from the body. Gently bend the knuckles to create a space between the palms. The fingertips, thumbs, and base of the palms are touching. Breathe normally. Notice what, if any, images or words appear. You may feel a sense of peace. Maybe an intention forms. It's okay if it doesn't. Repeat the intention to yourself three times.

3. **Anjali Mudra – Gesture of Reverence:** Bring the palms together. Allow the thumbs to press against the sternum. Repeat the intention three times. Feel it in the heart center. Breathe. Notice what arises.

4. **Padma Mudra – Gesture of the Lotus:** With hands in Anjali Mudra, move the index finger, middle finger, and ring finger away from each other so your hand forms the shape of the lotus flower. With an open heart and hands, feel the breath flow from the belly to the throat as you raise your hands up and overhead—your intention blossoms like the lotus flower. Repeat your intention once. Bring the hands back together into Anjali mudra. Allow them to rest at your heart center for a few breaths. Breathe and notice how you feel. Open your eyes.

After retiring from a corporate career and completing seven years of in-depth yoga teacher training, **Denyse** completed her Yoga Therapy Certification in 2017.

Since the pandemic, Denyse has offered virtual weekly yoga nidra sessions. She has augmented her yoga nidra studies by completing advanced certifications in iRest® Yoga Nidra and IAM™ Yoga Nidra.

In 2022, she began offering one-on-one bedside yoga therapy to oncology patients through the Inova Life with Cancer program.

Through her company, Lavender Om Wellness, LLC, she offers weekly yoga nidra, chair yoga, and chair yoga dance classes on Zoom. These practices have made her more relaxed and joyful.

Denyse volunteers for the Yoga Special Interest Group of the Society for Integrative Oncology and the Alzheimer's Research and Prevention Foundation's Yoga Advisory Council. As a certified Diabetes Prevention Program Lifestyle Coach, she lectures on how yoga tools may assist with Stress Management in type 2 diabetes prevention.

Denyse and her husband live in Virginia. They travel to visit family, enjoy different lands, and stroll on a beach enjoying warmth and sunshine. Denyse chats with Miranda from time to time.

Connect with Denyse:

Website: https://lavenderomwellness.com

Facebook: https://www.facebook.com/LavenderOmWellness

LinkedIn: linkedin.com/in/mdenyselefever

YouTube: https://www.youtube.com/channel/UC47CZzsYksSeKqrjDpJ1QmQ

Substack: https://mdenyselefever.substack.com

CHAPTER 6

The Secret to Joyful Living

HOW TO CURATE YOUR CURIOSITY SUPERPOWER

R. Scott Holmes

MY STORY

"I'm sorry,"

Grief thundered across my heart, threatening to break me open, and then, surprisingly, relief responded, the kind of peace I hadn't felt in decades. I had held my wife Moira's hand six months before as she took her last gasp of breath, losing her 20-year battle with breast cancer.

I'm really speaking with her!

The words came through Samantha the medium, but the words were my wife's.

"After Amanda passed, there was a hole so deep I couldn't feel love, and I was empty. I am so sorry."

Moira let me know she was with our daughter Amanda in the afterlife. She died at fifteen, wheelchair and bed-bound. Amanda now danced, skateboarded, sang, and was ecstatic in the afterlife.

The complexity of emotions I felt when grieving was isolating, stilting, and suffocating. Curiosity brought me to this first mediumship experience. Being open to the results with no expectations changed my life.

"Curiosity will conquer fear more than bravery will."
~ James Stephenson
(Instead of trying to summon up the courage, summon up curiosity.)

Love is the strongest force I've known and I would contend curiosity is the second most powerful. When comfortable in my own skin, people see me as rare, unusual, or just a pain in the ass. It may be their judgment that keeps them at a distance. Curiosity brings them closer.

What curiosity has been for me:

- Being called to meditate and find my lost soul parts at the altar of a forty-foot golden Buddha in a Burmese temple in Penang, Malaysia.

- Finding the All (Source) in walking meditation as I hiked the Himalayas in India near the Tibet border.

- Zip-lining down the mile-long mountain track on a dare with my granddaughter.

- Driving through the Swiss Alps in my sixtieth year on Earth with my high school friend, listening to the vibration of the mountain range and delighting in the vistas appearing around each corner and tunnel.

- Sitting across the beer-stained wooden table with my oldest friend, sipping a pint of Guinness in a Dublin pub and finding such gratitude in our fifty-plus-year friendship.

- Walking the desolate grounds of Mauthausen Concentration camp in Austria, the rock quarry and yards filled with fear and incredible sadness adding such weight to each step.

- My daily walk at sunrise while visiting my favorite beach on Amelia Island, Florida, delighting in the changes Mother Earth supplies each day.

- Sailing in Ha Long Bay, Vietnam, amazed at the people I met and how each form the next limestone island takes allows my imagination to fly free.

Demanding you seek greater knowledge of the world around you and of yourself.

Without curiosity how would we survive in this world? First by observation. As newborns we see our hands for the first time and wonder what they are, what they can do, and see they're even attached to our arms. Think of the wonder. With observation comes learning in the practice, movement, and beauty of our hands.

In its simplest form, think of the complexities in the act of walking. What it took to stand up, never mind placing one foot in front of the other while maintaining balance. Complex yet we don't think anything more of it after mastering the art.

It fuels independence. Without curiosity, we'd never know how to walk, how to stand up, how to run, how to do somersaults, or how to say the word "mother," the most beautiful word of all.

Being the oldest of four, I was expected to set the example, follow the rules, always show respect, never question, and always make decisions making my parents proud. Hmm. So exploring how leaves burnt when lit with a magnifying glass behind the garage was bad. Questioning having to go to Wednesday night choir practice instead of finishing our very competitive kickball game was argumentative. Building a seven-story, forty-foot-high tree house wasn't how I should spend my time. In my formative years I spent many a day grounded in my bedroom, but getting to explore my world was so rewarding.

When was the last time you didn't follow the rules?

"Curiosity is insubordination in its purest form."
~ Vladimir Nabokov

As a teenager posters of baseball stars and actresses were my bedroom wallpaper, but the most intriguing poster was "The Desiderata"—a treatise on how to navigate life. Its first line was "Go placidly amid the noise and the haste and remember what peace there may be in silence." It took me until 60 to fully understand what that meant—calm, grounded, at peace within myself without distraction, allowing me to be present.

"Once we believe in ourselves,
we can risk curiosity, wonder, spontaneous delight
or any experience that reveals the human spirit."

~ E. E. Cummings

Yes, curiosity rests on a fundamental belief that the human spirit is a blessing to be experienced, not protected.

Curiosity can be the fuel you use to move forward. I've been stuck at different phases of life, asking the ever-present question, "What is the meaning of life?" Monty Python summed it up best with their take. "Full of irony, angst, laughs, misunderstandings, and outright joy—life is how you perceive it to be."

Moira and I were in an emergency room for endless hours, waiting for answers that never came, while my eight-year-old daughter continued to spasm and seize. "Well, that's not something you see every day," as a whippet-like eighty-year-old man streaked past, baring all and eluding security. Dark humor then took over as my wife and I bantered with doctors and nurses, the moment so much lighter than it had been.

During some of life's scariest, most helpless times, humor mixed with curiosity was the life preserver of sanity in those perilous situations.

"Curiosity may have killed the cat, but it saved my ass."

~ Michael J. Fox

Finding ways to enhance and maintain our daughter's quality of life while she was alive was challenging and we constantly asked questions of the professionals around us. Embracing the situation and making the best of it, no matter how terrifying or overwhelming, allowed us to create the best answers. Looking back, I wouldn't change any decisions we made—no regrets. Looking at things from a different perspective gave us a lifeline to solve life as it unfolded.

Have you forgiven yourself for decisions made years ago?

Curiosity always questions and, in doing so, asks the toughest questions.

Curiosity fuels learning. I wondered why I felt other people's aches and pains, knowing what they felt and what they needed. Taking a Reiki course opened the floodgates to understanding. Excitement grew as I understood the world, how it's made up of vibrations, and how I could tap into them. Reiki II followed. Then Polarity Therapy, RYSE training, Reiki Master Certification, ThetaHealing, and dozens of courses, summits, Zooms, retreats, and certifications.

This all led me to a daily practice, a ritual, if you will. Although it takes work it's not work. Meditation, followed by yoga, enables me to start each day grounded and present, stabilizing my day so I can reach out to curiosity in all things.

> *"There is a moment in every child's life*
> *where a door opens and lets the future in."*
> ~ author Graham Greene

The goal is to be aware when a creative opportunity presents itself – instead of being so busy that we overlook it.

What wonder there is in understanding and knowing that the more answers I received, the more questions there were to ask.

Curiosity can be what allows judgment to leave. Judgment comes from your upbringing. The domestication of your imagination and wonder of life creates the box. Dogma in the form of school, church, and family's accepted values creates boundaries on right and wrong and who gets to set those standards.

Buddhism was considered foreign, meaning bad. Daoism, Confucianism, Hindu, Muslim, Judaism, and Orthodoxy of any sort were not understood or tolerated. There was one singular way to live life, and that was "How we do things!" I was told to follow without question and never really knew the why.

I read about different religions and points of view all through my teens. I have now come back to reading, learning, and understanding these religions and have traveled the world to understand how they manifest. Such a beautiful and expansive world we live in. And did you know there are millions of ways to live this life? Once your eyes are open, judgment leaves the high bench and doesn't cast its shadow anymore.

*"Life loves to be taken by the lapel and told,
'I am with you, kid. Let's go.'"*

~ Maya Angelou
(Curiosity isn't passive – it's an energetic embracing of life).

I'm only now living my best eighteen-year-old life!

Curiosity enables you to meet new people, no matter your age or status. When you're young, meeting people is expected. New friends, new situations, or changes in address lend themselves to reaching out. As an older adult, meeting new people can be a chore, almost painful, as life generally makes your daily world smaller as you walk the same path for so many years. Making different choices and embracing the new opens up pathways to meet those you didn't know.

What I came to find out was the secret I had been searching for all my life. No matter where you live on this Earth, all people want the same things, though it looks quite different.

- Safety and security for their loved ones in all its forms.
- To be loved and give love.
- And for peace in their lives.

Curiosity has become the foundation of my world and how it manifests. Curiosity is how I live with trust in this world. Because I know my authentic self, I can trust the world I live in.

Daily rituals of yoga, meditation, and healthy eating allow quiet amidst the noise and haste. In the quiet, I've come to know myself fully. When curiosity takes hold and is used on a daily basis, it can help define those deepest parts of you; that is when you become the curiosity.

*"I think, at a child's birth, if a mother could ask
a fairy godmother to endow it with the most useful gift,
that gift would be curiosity."*

~ Eleanor Roosevelt

We are all born innately curious. Without curiosity, we'd never grow and accept those changes. Did curiosity kill the cat? While we might not know the answer to that eternal question, I can honestly say that without curiosity, my life would be less than it could be.

"If you can let go of passion and follow your curiosity, your curiosity just might lead you to your passion."
~ Elizabeth Gilbert

Curiosity led me to become a student again. While teaching and coaching are part of what I do, learning is who I've come to be. While love is the strongest force known, curiosity holds a power of its own. If you're curious, please connect so we may find which path curiosity will take you.

THE PRACTICE

Let's start with the WHY:

Webster's Dictionary first defines curiosity as a concern, questioning, and inquisitiveness.

The opposite is indifference, apathy, and disinterest.

"Dad, can we just get you out of the bathtub and get dressed?" with irritation starting to creep up my neck.

Why does it take so long to do the simplest things?

Taking a breath to calm down, I asked my Dad what was making him hesitate. "I want to do this myself. Having to ask for help is demeaning and I can only move so fast."

My heart melted as I understood he felt diminished and helpless in his advanced years. My irritation transformed into compassion. Time stopped as I allowed however long it took for him to get dressed, only helping when he asked.

Find the why in all your relationships. You might be surprised by the answers you receive when you're curious enough to ask.

"Curiosity is a willing, proud, and eager confession of ignorance."
~ S. Leonard Rubinstein

Then the What:

Webster's second definition is rarity, wonder, and exotic.

The opposite is mutation, malformation, and monstrosity.

The calf was cresting. Blood, mucus, and fluids dripped all over the straw strewn across the stall. This great blob of wet hair, appendages, and guttural sounds was horrifying.

My grandfather finished pulling the calf upright, stroking its head with a towel. He gently encouraged the momma, telling her how proud he was of her.

It wasn't scary at all, it was wonderful! A new life was born.

What I thought of as disgusting was rare and exotic for a city boy. Then, I understood that what I thought was horribly monstrous had turned into a butterfly of emotion—beauty in its most natural state.

Is judgment your perspective, or is it curiosity?

"The power to question is the basis of all human progress."

~ Indira Ghandhi

Now the How:

Webster's third definition is idiosyncratic, individualism, and singularity.

The opposite is an oddity, eccentric.

"Damn it!" as coffee splashed all over my clean white shirt and multi-colored pastel tie. Nervous as I was for this interview, I had to laugh. As I pulled the car into a parking lot, my laughter started rolling, and I couldn't stop. Halfway to my appointment, I could choose to be late by going home and changing or continuing on.

Sopping up everything I could with used take-out napkins, I decided to be on time. Making it five minutes before they called my name, I strode in as if wearing a tuxedo. "This is not my usual style, but my coffee decided to disagree with me on the way over. It won the argument."

The three interviewers laughed as I caught them off guard and the interview went on as planned. In accepting what was, I turned a curiosity, a stained shirt and tie, into showing how I'd persevere through problems. What may initially be odd can make you stand out.

> *"It is always with excitement that I wake up in the morning wondering what my intuition will toss up to me, like gifts from the sea. Intuition tells the thinking mind where to look next."*
>
> ~ Jonas Salk
>
> (Creativity calls for us to honor intuitive nudges that are pointing us in new directions, pointing out new options.)

Finding and knowing your true, authentic self opens opportunities and gateways you could never imagine. Saying yes to curiosity is your superpower. Climb on the magic carpet of intuition and allow curiosity to take you further than you ever hoped. Let's take that journey together.

R. Scott Holmes is an intuitive energy practitioner and transformational coach using Reiki, Polarity Therapy, RYSE, ThetaHealing, and Find Your Voice coaching techniques to clear, ground, and align your energetic body. His specialty is collaborating with professional men and women, allowing them to heal and maintain their true paths in life.

He began walking in the holistic healing world when his wife of 39 years died after a 20-year battle with breast cancer. After years of caregiving for his daughter and wife, the world of coaching, healing, and energy opened. His soul journey has been to help heal others through one-on-one sessions, teaching, and volunteering.

Walk with him to find the rituals and daily practices enabling you to open those locked spaces. Allow your most authentic self to shine through. Embrace the life you are living.

Contact Scott for a free thirty-minute share to see if you, too, can unwrap the Pandora's box carried in your heart.

Connect with Scott:

Website: https://www.rscottholmes.com

Email: rscott_holmes@yahoo.com

Facebook: https://www.facebook.com/Scott.Holmes.31105674

Instagram: https://www.instagram.com/r.scottholmes

CHAPTER 7

Your Voice Matters; You Matter

DON'T LET ANYONE SHUT YOU DOWN

Carol Pilkington, CSA, Spiritual Counselor

MY STORY

I'm ten or eleven years old, and like many other nights eating dinner at the kitchen table, my father, mother, and older sister (by four and a half years) are talking as I listen.

My head turns side to side as the banter between my father and sister goes back and forth. But this night, I decided to chime in; something in the conversation piqued my interest, and I wanted to add my two cents. As I tried to get my point of view across, I heard this frustrated and annoyed voice roaring from my father, "Carol! You're saying a lot of words, but you aren't saying anything!" My heart felt like it had stopped beating, and I shut up immediately. I was devastated, and all I wanted to do was run and hide, but I couldn't move. I felt glued to the chair.

I can't remember attempting to participate in another meal-time conversation. I felt so stupid, and I wasn't going to take that risk again.

Little did I realize how much that incident would monitor what I would or wouldn't say for years to come.

In school, I rarely raised my hand to answer a question unless I was certain I knew it. Even then, I always hesitated. I never wanted to be wrong or appear stupid. In fifth grade, I was asked to go to the blackboard to solve a problem. On this one day, my sister's former fifth-grade teacher was substituting for my class. My sister was very smart, and I looked up to her. When I had trouble figuring out the problem, the teacher said something like, "Why can't you be more like your sister?"

Again, I was mortified and embarrassed in front of the whole class. Another confirmation that I should keep my mouth shut. My mother was like a lion protecting her cub. I found out years later that she went to the principal's office and stood up for me. I got to know and love my mother more for the human being she was after she died in 1974 than when she was alive. I never got to know her as adult daughters often do. I was 20 when she died of cancer.

A TURNING POINT

One thing these earlier experiences taught me was to listen and observe. My nature, in general, as far back as I can remember, has been to be quiet, reflective, and observant. I was in my early twenties when I was with a group of friends having philosophical conversations, and I was my usual quiet self. When all at once, I said something in response to what everyone was saying, and the room went quiet.

There was a popular commercial at the time with the slogan, "When E.F. Hutton speaks, everyone listens." There were people gathered and chattering, and when E.F. Hutton spoke, everyone stopped and turned their heads. Well, it was that kind of moment. After I spoke, it was as though there was nothing else to say. Someone said to me, "You're so quiet, but wow, when you do say something, it's like you wrap up everything we've been talking about in such a clear, succinct way; how do you do that?!" I heard everyone; I understood everyone and summed all of it up in a nutshell. I literally blew their mind.

It was the first time I realized that people heard and understood what I had to say, and it was the spark of a new journey for me. *Maybe people do want to hear what I have to say, and my voice does matter; I matter.*

There was more evidence of this throughout my career in IT (Information Technology). I never rose to the level of manager (not for lack of merit but for not having a college degree), nor was I ever officially a supervisor. However, time and time again, high-level directors and company officers came to me, over my direct managers, for advice and opinion.

STILL MORE WORK TO DO

Even though I had these wonderful moments when I felt my voice mattered, I was still shy about opening up, especially about things that mattered to me; I was afraid of being crushed. As I look back, I recall there was resentment. On the one hand, I wanted to say something but wouldn't out of fear and rejection. On the other hand, I got upset when no one would ask me what I thought, or I felt ignored and invisible.

What resulted was me interrupting or trying to insert my opinions at inappropriate times, which disrupted the flow. Or, I stewed in silence, feeling I wasn't being seen, with that old trigger of not feeling like my voice mattered (that I didn't matter) kicking in. It was a no-win all the way around. Afterward, I admonished and shamed myself for my inappropriateness, which only made things worse and caused me to shut down even more.

You know when you are sitting around talking and whoever is speaking will often make eye contact with each person in the group? Well, there was this one person in the group who never seemed to make eye contact with me, and it made me feel as though I was not part of the conversation and that I was invisible. The topic would change, and I'd get pissed off that I did not get to say what I wanted on the matter discussed before. This one time I thoroughly embarrassed myself and yelled, "I can never get a word in edge-wise." I stood up to walk out the door. And this person said, "If you walk out, you don't get to come back." It was a major teaching moment. More about this later.

"WHAT YOU SEEK IS SEEKING YOU"

That is the last line of a famous Rumi quote and I've experienced it to be true throughout my life. I took EST (Erhard Seminar Training) in the early 80s, which was great but not enough. It would be another 20 years before Jim, my best friend and teacher, came into my life and took me to levels of consciousness and evolution I couldn't even imagine. I was ready. He and I met through a Personals ad on Yahoo. So, yes, he was seeking me too. He was new to Los Angeles and trying to get his footing in a new state and city. My life changed forever the day we met. He was a Jungian therapist who used astrology in his clinical practice and was also trained and experienced in metaphysics and mysticism. He couldn't practice in California as a therapist without practically starting all over again by getting the hours he needed to be licensed here. He'd already had 35 years in clinical and private practice, so he wasn't about to do that. He decided to become a teacher of astrology and metaphysics. I've been blessed to reap the benefits of his vast and eclectic knowledge and teachings. Not only did I learn about astrology but also Kabbalah, The Golden Dawn, and so much more. I learned and also had transformative experiences that changed me at a DNA level.

One of the things I learned, which might sound counterintuitive at first, was to exaggerate that trigger and play it out. Once I became aware of this deep trigger of feeling that my voice didn't matter and how that played out in my life in all the ways described above, I had to make it real and see it fully from all angles.

Remember the story I told you above regarding not being acknowledged in conversations? Well, this exercise that I'm about to share with you, cured all that and the person I referred to was Jim.

Jim would say, "Once you see the trigger in its entirety, what are you going to do about it?" He would say, "What you can do is consciously amplify and exaggerate it."

This is the fun part, if you can believe it. Because once you see something fully, it no longer has its claws in you and you can begin to consciously play with it. I decided to start a networking group (where I was the leader, of course). And what happens when you're the leader up in front of the room? Everyone listens to you; you have a captive audience. Nothing could've been better or more fun.

This exercise turned into a lifelong growth spurt and changed me on so many levels. I no longer craved attention; I no longer felt invisible; I no longer felt I didn't have a voice. It gave me the freedom to speak when I really had something to contribute to a conversation rather than blurt things out at inappropriate moments that didn't make sense. I enjoyed being able to listen intently and know that I had a choice to speak or not. I governed my choice based on whether or not I felt what I had to say would move the conversation forward or whether it was a righteous opinion I wanted to assert to satisfy my self-importance. To be brutally honest with oneself is key as it saves any repercussions and negative consequences afterward.

The other thing that came out of doing this exercise and becoming aware of this deeply embedded trigger was that no one was doing anything to me. I created my own misery and suffering, and I am the author of my own reality.

THE PRACTICE

Try it for yourself and see what happens. Pick something you know triggers the heck out of you (spontaneously gets you viscerally riled seeming out of the blue), and every time it raises its ugly head and disrupts your life, you want to hide in embarrassment and shame because you've caught yourself in this situation yet again. See how it has played out in your life in all its forms. Again, like I said, you have to be willing to be brutally honest with yourself and finally want to exorcise this puppy.

Example: Has anyone ever called you a whiney, complaining baby? Have you heard it more than once and from different sources in one way or another? Take that and look at the nature of what drives it. And when you've tapped into it, see it fully.

Give every facet of it the light of day, taking it out of the shadows. There is no room for shame and blame here; it's pure observation, no judging. Otherwise, it just digs its claws into you deeper. Instead, this is where you get to see it and consciously play with it, exaggerate it, and have fun with it.

Write an elaborate story about it if you like; if you're in the company of people you know and they're the ones who called you whiney, play it up. Don't wilt and shrivel up. You'll have fun, and they will, too. And they'll begin to see a change in you. I guarantee this deeper trigger will begin to loosen its grip on you, if not immediately, over time, and you'll feel freer from it than you could ever imagine. It might actually rear its head in other ways later on, but you'll catch it quicker and be less inclined to hide from it.

If you find that a particular deep trigger is a bit too much to tackle, be observant of other things on a smaller scale and practice and play until you're ready to take on the deeper things. You might even discover that they're connected.

In closing, we tend to take ourselves way too seriously. When we become aware of our triggers and play with them, we know we're on the right track, and often, we see how far we've come in the rearview mirror. When we become aware of something that used to trigger us and now tends to roll off our shoulders, we can see how far we've come. The more courage we have to make the unconscious conscious, the higher we raise our self-awareness and awareness of others.

Carol Pilkington, CSA, Spiritual Counselor

With over 30 years of combined training in spirituality, astrological counseling, personal development, and deep transformational work, Carol works with high-functioning, high-achieving entrepreneurs and executives who are living in a state of anxiety, depression or grief/loss, showing them how to move through and beyond these human conditions so they can live with more joy purpose and meaning.

Carol, a graduate of the Sher Institute of Astrology & Metaphysics, was trained by a Jungian therapist in multiple disciplines such as transpersonal astrology, Kabbalah, General Semantics (forerunner to NLP), and many others, Landmark Education Worldwide, and holds a certification in End-of-Life Care from the Twilight Brigade through the Veterans Administration. She is also an ordained non-denominational Minister. Carol also is a CSA (Certified Senior Advisor).

Carol is twice an Amazon best-selling and an International best-selling author. She has spoken on numerous podcasts and radio shows and appeared on multiple stages with the likes of Beverly D'Angelo, Glenn Morshower, Jack Canfield, and Suzy Prudden (Itty Bitty Publishing).

Carol is also a Senior Owner/Partner of The Wellness Universe, a one-stop resource for all things related to mind/body/spirit, which is committed to happy, healthy, healed humans leading to peace globally and provides wellness programs for corporations and organizations.

Philanthropic endeavors include being on the Advisory Board of the Foundation for Senior Services, a resource hub for all things related to Seniors and their families to help them age well with dignity, and facilitating workshops for seniors and their loved ones.

Carol loves just hanging out with close friends, playing board games, or watching Star Trek.

Connect with Carol:

https://www.carolpilkington.com

https://www.movingbeyondgrief.com

https://linktr.ee/awareandconscious

https://www.linkedin.com/in/solutionsforyou/

https://www.facebook.com/carol.pilkington

Books:

Your Amazing Itty Bitty Book of Astrology:
https://a.co/d/98wpLRr

Your Amazing Itty Bitty WPN Expert Compilation Book:
https://a.co/d/aiZroLe

CHAPTER 8

The Unexpected Gift of Infertility

KNOW YOUR BACKSTORY, HEAL YOUR LIFE

Jennifer K. Sproul, Founder, Graceing Agefully™

MY STORY

"You can't be *my* daughter," she chirped.

I told Mom that I needed major surgery to clear a blockage in my fallopian tubes.

She *never* had trouble conceiving. On the contrary, pregnancy was too often unexpected or inconvenient in her experience and my older sisters'. Too many had become pregnant at inconvenient times.

Maybe I was one of the inconveniences given I came when she and my father were almost 40. In the 1950s, 40 was **old** for childbirth.

She didn't flinch, knowing I'd take this step with a prospective father who was frequently unemployed, a cinematographer, and an artist. We weren't married after seven years of "living together in sin," as they say.

Her uncharacteristic ease with my unmarried status felt more like resignation than acceptance.

I was 37, still unmarried and in love.

I'm not a whole woman without a man who loves me enough to commit. I'm not a whole woman if I can't have children. These thoughts ran on a constant loop in my head.

I met him while he ruminated in despair. His brilliant, uber-accomplished, feminine feminist ex-wife tore out a chunk of his heart by cheating on him and leaving, never delivering the promised child he longed for.

This was my chance. I could fill the missing piece in his heart that would complete his love for me and, in turn, complete me as a woman. His only condition for marriage was my willingness and ability to give him a child.

It's fair. I'm defective merchandise until the surgery that will fix me.

A warm, soft cocoon of flannel sheets and down welcomed me at home.

The wound in my belly, a throbbing scarlet dividing line between my upper and lower halves, reminded me that the mission was accomplished!

It was worth it. I'm on the way to being a whole woman.

"The surgery was a success!" I heard those glorious words whispered in my semiconscious ears by the surgeon who made me a whole woman while I slept. I was finally worthy of love and marriage.

I fell into a deep sleep; visions of pregnancy and being a wife and mother danced in my head and into my dreams.

The woman I modeled evolved, and I didn't get the memo. Things changed from when my parents and siblings were young. I wasn't updated!

My siblings were born during and at the end of World War II. I was the youngest, the last of five, born six years after the youngest. I have three older sisters. They were the examples for me of women.

I loved dressing up in their cast-off prom dresses. I pictured myself wearing lipstick and makeup, stockings, and coiffed hair. I felt like a princess with spaghetti straps, a tight bodice, a full skirt, and high heels on the arm of a handsome, popular, nice boy. I couldn't wait!

Until the summer of '66, when my world collapsed.

"We're moving to Connecticut!" she told me, hopeful it would be good news for her only child still at home.

She continued, "It's only an hour away, and your father won't have to pay the New York state taxes. In Connecticut, there is no state income tax."

And I care about that why?

That year, my last sibling at home graduated from the high school in the town where we lived for ten years, a.k.a. my entire life. They were a unit. I was a supplement.

When I was born, my parents were unaware my birth introduced them to a whole new era of parenting. They probably thought they were off the hook. They probably thought they had mastered the parenting thing with my four siblings.

Little did they know I'd be a different kind of project. It was a new era, and it came with an entirely new version of women.

Meanwhile, all I knew was I was being surgically extracted from my family unit and my safe community that knew them and me. I was uprooted and transplanted a world away from the only home I knew.

I was 11—the time when girls became women. My image of being a woman was my dress-up fantasy of proms, dates, and cheerleading that led to engagements, weddings, and children!

I was not happy.

"This is not fair! All my friends are here. I'm coming back every week for the rest of my life!" I ranted to Mom.

In Connecticut:

What's with this house?

Our home was a beautiful, big Victorian home with three acres, a barn, and big, shady maple trees.

This new house had no upstairs, ugly designer colors, and no sidewalks!

Ugh. I hate it!

I landed hard with an attitude on day one!

I was dropped into a new era and world at a pivotal moment.

In this new world, the dress code was casual.

Blue jeans replaced pressed crisp chinos for boys, and girls wore them too!

Sneakers replaced penny loafers.

Pantyhose replaced garter belts and stockings.

Hemlines moved way up the leg.

Home parties and school dances (not proms) were the norm for social gatherings.

There was no downtown in the new world as there was in my small town home.

We traveled in packs. Everyone went to college. High school was now college prep for *all* boys and *all* girls.

I was dropped into a foreign land, and nothing looked familiar or like home.

Nobody dresses like a princess, ever. I'm not going on dates like my sisters.

When a senior boy asked me out on a date in my freshman year, it involved a car he drove, and Mom wouldn't let me.

"You don't know what boys will want to do if they get you in a car!"

It didn't occur to her that you couldn't go anywhere without a car in this new place.

On my 13th birthday, October 26, 1967, everything happened in one day.

My first date was a group hay ride with a boy who invited me, my first kiss (forgettable at best), *and* I got my period.

Wow! The big day felt *meh!*

Back at school, they're saying, "You need to prepare for college."

Why? I don't need a college degree, I don't want to be a doctor or a lawyer, and I don't know what I want to BE except a popular girl and probably a wife and a mother.

Neither of my parents had college degrees. My brother did, but he was a boy. None of my sisters had four-year degrees.

My father was surprised when my teachers told him, "She's good in math and science." He didn't think girls could be good at those things. Boys and men, yes, but girls?

I was confused. I heard messages that I wasn't like a woman. I read them to mean I wasn't feminine. That story became a tape in my head that played on a continuous loop.

You are not enough. You are not feminine. You are not an attractive woman. You don't fit in. You are not right.

I would *work* at being enough. I wanted to fit in.

I didn't want the world to know I wasn't the woman I thought I should be.

Meanwhile, Mom was my only connection to home who came with me to this new foreign place. I needed her to listen to my rants. I needed her to love me, understand me, and feel my pain with me.

Instead, I got her diminishing, threatened self-esteem, pushing away my teen angst.

Now I can look back and separate my melodrama from her menopausal survival drama about parenting a teenage girl in a new era and a new world. Dad was a pilot and away much of the time, so she had to navigate those turbulent seas solo.

In retrospect, I realize we were both unmoored and seeking safe harbor in a roiling sea of uncertainty. We were too absorbed in our stories to help each other.

That's my coming-of-age story, the story that landed me in my **illusive** cocoon after surgery—the cocoon of a whole, albeit outdated, model of a woman.

This story began as I was falling deeply asleep in the peace of believing I was finally enough.

Then, I woke up.

My mother was at *my* home to take care of *me*.

*Why am I taking care of **her**?* I thought.

Why am I girding my loins to keep them from falling out on the floor (that's what abdominal surgery left me feeling like) *so I can make dinner for Mom and my partner?* She was too tired after an afternoon glass of wine, and she wasn't comfortable cooking in our kitchen. He had an exotic palate. She'd never be able to make anything he approved of, let alone eat.

"Dinner in a Dish" from the *Life Magazine* cookbook series of that name was a dish that would surely be the target of his merciless (and hilarious) ridicule, with the bull's eye on me right behind.

That's okay, I thought. I preferred enduring the searing pain of standing over the stove to the searing pain of his look of disgust when presented with something my mother might've set before him.

As I write this, I feel ashamed.

I can't believe I let a man define my worth, mistaking it for love.

Months after surgery made me believe I was a whole woman, we still weren't pregnant. I hoped my partner would concede to marriage despite my infertility, given my valiant effort to remedy the situation.

Thirty years later, this is cracking me open wider than ever.

My pursuit of love and acceptance through motherhood ended when I learned once again my fallopian tubes had scarred, blocking the tiny channel to my wholeness, my value, and my worth.

I felt my value as an unmarried 37-year-old with an average record of business success was worth less than the other women I knew who were doing that *and* married with children.

My partner reminded me of that. *OUCH.*

People asked, "Why aren't you married?" I made excuses and apologies. I dismissed them: "I'm in a long-term relationship. I don't need a piece of paper to seal our commitment!"

LIAR, LIAR PANTS ON FIRE!

I wanted that paper! That was proof! That was the validation I needed. I was too ashamed to admit it to my friends and acquaintances.

I was too ashamed to admit it to myself.

My partner and I drifted apart as we navigated the new terrain.

I snapped out of the euphoric haze of my fantasy of love, marriage, motherhood, and womanhood when I was promoted. The promotion required that I move.

"I don't want to move," he said, "I like it here."

He wouldn't consider moving with me. The move was less than an hour from our home and in the same metropolitan area. Ironic? I think so.

The raw truth of my misguided, eager acceptance of a man's commoditization of me finally hit me like a lightning bolt.

Our relationship dissolved. Like salt in warm water, it was easy. He tried to keep a hold on me emotionally while he pulled away physically and left the country for his homeland for nine months. He returned with his new wife and baby son in tow.

Lightning bolt #2.

His mission was accomplished!

Looking back today, I'm shocked.

This blows a lid off my still partially locked-down heart. I'm exposing my soft inner core to you, the world, and myself for the first time.

I'm turning 70 this year, dear reader; it's never too late to heal and move forward.

Writing this and piecing together the backstory helped me understand why I did what I did. It allowed me to forgive myself.

It showed me the breadcrumb trail that brought me to where I am today, and that is where and how change happens.

The gift was clear when the lightning bolt struck. I woke up. I dodged a bullet!

I saw myself as a whole woman for the first time. I am many things that don't include being a wife and mother. I AM smart. I AM funny. I AM strong. I AM enough. I AM a woman (hear me roar?). Just kidding.

Like magic, I attracted a man who sees me for who I AM. I wasn't convinced immediately. It took time for me to trust. It took time to open my heart to love. He was persistent, unwavering in his attraction. He wasn't playing games. He wasn't playing hard to get. He was open with his affection. It took the old me a long time to vacate the premises. She still haunts the outer rooms of my psyche. I'm still a work in progress.

Five years later, we married—me for the first time at 45. He has a wonderful son from a previous marriage and didn't want any more children. After we were together for a few months, he told me, "If you want to adopt a child, I think you would be a great mother and I'll go there with you."

The fact is, I didn't need it. His words struck me like another bolt of lightning—*he's the one.* The difference is that I know I AM worthy of love.

I AM enough.

THE PRACTICE

Writing my backstory illuminated the path I took to arrive where I am today.

I learned along the way that when it comes to change, we must start where we are. Starting where we are requires awareness and acceptance. It requires being present.

All my life I looked ahead. I always saw what I thought I wanted to be in the distance. What I saw was what I believed I was *expected* to be to be *enough*.

All the time I spent trying, striving to be what I thought I *wanted* to be, I was **not present**. I *thought* I was not whole. I thought I was not enough.

The ramifications of thinking we aren't enough are profound.

Thinking we're not enough gives rise to behaviors like numbing, distracting, and resisting. These behaviors set us on a path to addictive behaviors and chronic health issues. The further we go, the more difficult it is to come to a state of wellness.

EMPTY YOUR MIND ON THE PAGE

"Morning Pages" changed my life. "Morning Pages" is a tool created by Julia Cameron in *The Artist's Way*. First thing in the morning, I write on paper with a pen. I write what's in my head. It's not always coherent; it doesn't matter. Articulating the noise in my monkey mind with a pen on paper has power. A daily habit reveals recurring thoughts. Themes come up and show me what I need to work on.

Morning pages were my gateway to awareness. I expressed thoughts on paper I hadn't been willing to face. Once pages are written, I feel clear and calm to start my day. As I saw the same messages repeated, I became aware. I learned my story by reading my journal as if it were written by someone else.

Morning pages were my gateway to writing. The pages weren't for publication. I loved the process. When my mind was clear, I found I'd write as if it was channeled. The ideas coming through had a clear path to the page. I wrote easily and knew when it was time to stop. I read what I wrote afterward, and it felt like I hadn't written it.

It's an out-of-body experience. I continue to learn from journaling.

TELL YOUR STORY IN DETAIL

We live our stories every day, and we believe them. Our stories are records of history, experiences, trauma, delight, fear, and love. They combine to create the belief system that programs our lives.

Imagine a vinyl record with grooves. The grooves can be scratched, and the output changes. The grooves can be deep ruts. We fall in and repeat behaviors. We change and scratch the groove.

Tell your story in detail. Write it. Go back and refine it. Go deeper. Read to someone who has no idea what your story is about. You'll hear things you hadn't thought about before. You'll connect the dots. Suddenly, you see the pieces you thought were different are the same. You see patterns you didn't recognize before. You see your limiting beliefs.

Limiting beliefs are what hold you back. When you reverse engineer the path that got you where you are, you see what you can change. You'll know why you did what you did. You'll see why you do what you do. You can forgive yourself.

FORGIVE YOURSELF

I forgive myself by *accepting* my mistakes and missteps. I can write it in a journal or share it with a friend and it's out there. Once it's exposed it's in the past. I move on.

When you know how you got here and forgive yourself for past mistakes, you're free. You change the recording, etch a new groove, and rewrite your program.

You are on the path to self-actualization.

Jennifer K. Sproul is the founder of Graceing Agefully™, a platform she launched in July 2022 to "change the *culture* of aging."

In October 2024, she turns 70.

"We become what we think and believe. If we believe getting old is a downhill descent to death after age 60, it will be. If we focus on deepening self-awareness we can reprogram our minds to override the negative conditioning and limiting beliefs of the culture. We will thrive. We can have a very long life and health span. I believe Baby Boomers are the first generation with the opportunity to move the needle on average lifespan to triple digits (100+)."

Jennifer walks the walk (or runs the run as the case may be!).

At age 50 she left a successful 20-year career as a corporate sales executive. She started over and found success as a Realtor®. At age 58 she ran her first full marathon (26.2 miles). At age 60 she realized she could live to be 120+ which meant she was only halfway. At 67 she began to write. She wrote and published two chapters in Amazon bestselling collaborations published by Brave Healer Productions in 2022 and 2023.

This chapter in *Gifts of Wisdom, Practices for Healing and Empowerment* is her third.

In July 2022, she launched Graceing Agefully™ from which she publishes a monthly blog to inspire Baby Boomers to become Baby *Bloomers*!

In October 2023, she spoke on the TEDx Bethesda Women stage.

Title: Stop Trying, Start Living.

Connect with Jennifer:

Website: https://graceingagefully.com

Facebook: https://www.facebook.com/graceingagefully

LinkedIn:

https://www.linkedin.com/company/86878005/admin/feed/posts/

She can be reached via email: jennifer@graceingagefully.com

CHAPTER 9

Opening Inward

LIVING LIFE THROUGH BODY PRESENCE

Janine Savient, The Heart Lady

MY STORY

I noticed him immediately. He was new at school; this was his first day. He sat by himself, knees drawn up, arms folded around them like he was hiding inside himself. My heart responded to the deep sadness I felt as I observed him.

Always guided by my body/heart awareness, I walked across the playground to welcome him, as this is who I am.

From my earliest memory, I felt different from those around me. The reason was that I was deeply aware of life, not just physically but also vibrationally. I did not just know myself in life; I knew life was in me; I felt it energetically in every moment.

I was sensitive to the beauty and trauma of my life. As an empathic, compassionate observer, I understood all I felt was being communicated in response to my external experiences. I realized others around me didn't experience their lives similarly. Life didn't appear to touch them with the depth it did me, or if it did, they seemed unable to recognize this.

Because of my sensitivity, I regularly needed time to be alone, away from the noise of having three boisterous brothers and a very practical, down-to-earth father. I loved them dearly and understood from an early age that my choice was to join them in their boisterousness or get trampled in the rush of their lives. When I could, I did, and when I felt depleted or overwhelmed, I retreated into my still inner space.

This was how I knew life for years—all in or all out of it.

Unrecognized yet by me at that age, I already knew the power of presence. Being still, shutting out the noise of the external world, and being inward rejuvenated me, bringing me a sense of more profound calm and self-awareness.

My mother was the gentle, guiding, loving energy in the mix, and from her motherly love, I learned the lightness, love, and laughter of life.

However, I always knew I wasn't a good fit with my family or this life experience. From the beginning, I saw through all the systems of this world and often questioned the reasons behind what I witnessed.

The differences between me and most others were obvious in my childhood. Most appeared content living within this world, which, to me, made no sense. It was like I lived in a completely different reality.

The teacher's duster hit me hard on the back of my head. I got caught daydreaming in class, as often happened.

The thud startled me, and feeling bruised, it brought me sharply back into my body and awareness of the classroom.

Ouch, that hurt!

Rubbing the back of my neck where the duster connected with me, I thought, *OMG, this is so boring! How much longer before the lunch bell goes?*

I looked longingly through the window outside to the grassy, sun-filled playground.

I wanted to run and play, journey into my imagination, and delight with beautiful light beings that came on the rays of the sunshine. I wanted to feel the earth beneath my bare feet, climb trees, smell flowers, and be with the elemental beings whose job it was to look after the natural world. That was my world, too—not this crazy, regimental world of rules and regulations I felt stifled by every day.

My world was a multi-layered reality, and through these layers (these inner doorways of connectedness), I felt deeply alive and learned from beautiful beings within those worlds how the frequency of love in me was the creative force within everything.

Being forced to live in a world known only on the physical level by those around me was very challenging. And since no one in school ever taught us about any other level, I found it a complete waste of time.

"Who the heck started her off again?" was often the frustrated shout by the teacher as I found something hysterically funny and laughed so hard I cried. I was a loud, proud laugher. A belly laugh was something I learned with my mother, often to my father's frustration, which just made us laugh even louder. A feeling of mischief always encouraged our shared laughter to get deeper and louder.

Laughter, I found, was a perfect distraction from the tedious classroom applications.

To be in joy, fun, laughter, and playfulness was my true vibrational frequency. I thrived in anything that lifted me into these lighter frequencies.

For me, every physical aspect of life was more about the vibrational level than the physical representation of it. Yet, I was a child, and adults knew better, apparently. There were a few of them who tried to mold me into who they thought I should be.

Therefore, in my teens, I became a rebel. I had enough of being told who I ought to be and how life really was. I was told, "It's not your imaginary world." They taught me it was all about the real physical world.

I felt empowered by stretching or breaking the rules and often did so.

There were also times when I fell into a deep sadness with how this world was for me, and in these heavy periods, I often felt like leaving, simply ending my life and exiting this dense reality.

Over the next few years, I lost myself in many unhealthy pastimes, rebelling, pushing against life and ignoring my deeper awareness. Eventually, however, life would spit me out again, and I would rise back into my deeper knowing, pick myself up and for a while at least, I would remember that stillness within me and how I could detach from the external world for a time.

What a journey it was, what a roller coaster of emotions. I deepened into confusion as I grew through my teens, and self-doubt grew.

No one sees or understands the real me. No one knows how I truly feel and how life is for me. Why am I so different from everyone else? These thoughts often ran through my head.

I also had a growing disconnection with my body. To me, my body was always cumbersome, a heavy part that kept me here in this harsh and false reality. From an early age, I knew how to leave it and fly out into far-off places that weren't a part of this world. And so I did—often.

One night while lying quietly, I received a message: *You can leave this life if you want to. If you stay, you're going to have to take care of yourself, however.*

I had deeply neglected my body, apparently, and now it was time to learn a new level of self-care.

I stayed and focused on why my body was so darn important. I knew I'd regret leaving before fully understanding why I had even landed here. It wasn't time to leave yet.

Over the past 15 years, I've recognized and remembered the importance of the body and what an amazing temple it is for my consciousness to play in. In recent years, I learned more about presence and being fully in my body, plus the multi-dimensional experiences offered when I take great care of my body and love it deeply. It was designed to hold magnificence (which is who we all are). As I journey from the thinking mind into my beautiful body, I realize, piece by piece, the truth of my magnificence and all I forgot while living in separation from that truth.

What is presence?

To know what presence is, you must first understand the lack of presence. Most human beings haven't realized their lack of presence in their own life.

Humans have been so deeply conditioned since birth to listen outwardly, to hear who and what they are from external sources. These sources include religion, the educational and medical systems, governments, corporate marketing, all advertising, television and movie theaters, and books and magazines.

Most are so conditioned that they've forgotten how to be in their body, in the moment, in silence, in stillness, with no external stimuli suggesting, inviting, or telling them who they are and what their best choices should be.

Inwardly, you find a deep connection where no outer authority tells you who you are and what you should like, do, be, or feel.

Deep inner connection is where you come into the loving presence of yourself and grow your trust in your inner knowing of what feels right.

A lifetime of being told what you should and shouldn't do and what is best for you programmed you into living on autopilot, often believing you're free to make your own choices while being subconsciously steered down particular avenues. This influence is so subtle yet powerful that most never realize their choices are heavily manipulated.

Becoming present brings you into feeling life with your body/heart awareness, through your inner authority, choosing for yourself, saying no in the face of external authority, or yes if you agree. This is a somewhat controversial subject in these times; however, never has there been a more powerful opportunity to come into presence and live your life your way.

This is you, bringing change to a world that is so ready for it.

When you begin the journey out of your head and into your body, you are becoming present. Your mind, ideas, and beliefs keep you separated from your deep, true knowing, which is found as you take the 'inner journey,' facing yourself through truth and transparency as the parts born from within these ideas and beliefs are acknowledged, accepted, and released.

Through this inner journey, you feel a new depth to yourself, as if you are multi-layered and not simply a physical being. You feel a growing pull that calls you into silence, stillness, and what can only be described as a deepening spaciousness within you. This is your conscious awareness deepening as you come into the presence of yourself in the now-moment experience.

You show up in life as the deep observer. You notice the smallest things that touch you at a depth not realized before.

In becoming conscious of the moment, all physical senses are tuned in. You notice, observe, and feel the moment—you're present, and as you become aware that the moment has a new depth, you also notice that the depth is being realized within you as you observe yourself in the moment.

YOU, AS THE OBSERVER, ARE OBSERVING YOURSELF AS THE EXPERIENCER.

In presence, your awareness is in your body, and you can feel the subtle energies as your outer and inner senses become more acute; now, all you perceive around you is being felt within you.

Your deepening awareness brings you more and more into the moment, and in presence, you feel your body as a finely tuned instrument, a radar, receiver, and antenna that receives and translates all the moment holds.

In this state of being, you take in far more through deepening observation. You're acutely aware of the information/data coming into your body and the translation of this information into feelings moving through you. That largely untapped place within you where your deepest knowing comes from, is present to show you that moment in the finest detail. It's as if you already knew—because you do!

It takes practice to become present in your life. You're used to being led, guided, and told how your life is, through your mind and by outside authority.

THE PRACTICE (PART ONE)

Right now, take a deep breath into your belly. Feel your stomach and chest extend as you fill with that breath, and feel your body soften as you release the breath. Repeat this breathing, filling and releasing a few more times, keeping your complete awareness on your breathing and body as you do so. This breathing is done comfortably for you and becomes deeper and slower as you are in it.

Again, feel your body softening, tension leaving as you relax into the moment. Your eyes are open but softly gazed, your shoulders and face relaxed, and you feel peaceful but alert and aware of your body.

Now, fix your soft gaze on a point in front of you. Your attention is within your body and not on the point of your gaze. Through your awareness, feel your breath expanding within you, noticing your body feeling lighter and more spacious.

Keeping your eyes open and gently fixed keeps you physically in your body in this moment.

Next, say with authority, "Here now," commanding your whole self to be present, feeling a new level of acute alertness or hypersensitivity, as if more of you has now dropped in.

In this practice, do not move your eyes to look around yourself, which will come later once you master being present within your body. This, now, is all about feeling the depth and spaciousness within you. In presence, the feeling of being physical dissolves, and you become the vibrational field itself.

By this stage, your skin feels extremely sensitive. Any bare skin is hyper-alert, as if it is aware of the vibrational field touching it, as indeed it is.

Be with this feeling. You may feel light, soft, and fluid. And rather than you being in your life experience, you may feel you've become the experience itself in this moment—pure feeling, no edges, no separation, simply spacious flow, and hypersensitivity.

The practice right now is about you being consciously in your body and feeling it as a vibrational receiver, nothing more.

The next part comes once you feel completely open and relaxed with this part of the practice.

You may have noticed there is no place for your thinking mind within this practice. No thoughts, ideas, beliefs, or expectations enter. All those parts relate to external programming and have held you in the limiting belief that your consciousness, your physical body, and heart awareness are separate rooms within the mansion of your being. They are not.

The external world taught you that your thinking mind needs to be constantly fed and stimulated to achieve your highest potential.

When, in fact, your highest potential is realized as you move deeper into your inner awareness, whereby the possibilities and opportunities you contain in your deeper knowing open to you.

Know that the further in you go, the further out into your life experience you expand, bringing you new doorways to enter and new choices on offer.

This is you coming home into your deepest, greatest, most incredible truth of who and what you are as the high-frequency being of pure love.

Begin when you're ready to move into the next part of the practice.

THE PRACTICE (PART TWO)

You're fully aware now of how easily your body softens into the vibrational field, becoming one with it. You feel the vibrational flow through yourself automatically with your focus on your breathing, body, the softening of your thinking mind, and the slowing down and stillness of the moment you're in.

Start softly moving your eyes and realizing all that sight gives you. Breathe in and feel the colors, notice the shapes and textures, and observe the movements around you, holding your awareness in your body's radar the whole time. Keep aware of the feelings moving through you as your eyes move and your inner and outer senses switch on.

Again, as the observer, you feel you, as the experiencer, in this moment.

Open into your sense of smell now; what can you smell in this moment? Register this without dwelling in thought. Is it fresh? Is it stale? Is there any smell at all? Notice and move on. Open into hearing; listen deeply. What can you hear? Bring the sounds in and allow the vibration of the sounds to flow through you; they will generally become one sound after a few seconds. Feel this sound in your body as pure vibration. Sometimes, you may need to close your eyes briefly as you register the sounds or smells.

If you feel like bringing in touch, do so. Touch deliberately, lightly, and consciously, registering the textures. The same for taste if relevant in this moment.

Presence becomes a very sensual practice. It means being fully aware of yourself in the moment in relation to the external world and your inner reality.

This practice can also be done with no external influence. By closing your eyes and being in your body and your feelings, you allow yourself to experience a layer of reality that is often unknown until it is.

With practice, you live your life more and more from this deeper awareness, noticing that you no longer feel fully met on the level of the surface, shallow world of thought.

Moving through your life in presence means experiencing yourself, with your heart wide open to feeling your way and your body open and tuned in to the subtle energies and vibrational frequencies of the external experience and internal reality. You're returning to your true nature as a feeling being rather than what you have been told you are: a thinking being.

Thinking has a place, but it's secondary to feeling your way in life.

Your body/heart awareness always has your highest good as its outcome through all decisions made from this inner place, for this is the communication center with your highest or Soul Self, your direct line with Source Energy.

This is the truth of who you are.

Janine Savient came into this life wide awake to knowing herself and life as multi-layered realities. She can see through the physical layer and into the vibrational/energetic realities beneath, which has brought with it an awareness of life as a felt experience. Through the tutelage of benevolent beings from other realities, Janine learned that love is this universe's fundamental and all-creative energy.

Over the years, her gifts of clairvoyance, claircognizance, and clairempathy have deepened acutely. By knowing herself as a being of pure love, she understands who she is and why she came.

Using her natural gifts, ability as an intuitive visionary, and body/heart awareness, Janine walks beside the inner traveller in support of their journey home into their heart of pure love.

Janine knows that this reality is undergoing the greatest change now and that this change is rising within every human. She fully sees the person's beauty beneath the stories, ideas, and beliefs they hold, and through the purity of love's presence, she supports them in realizing their most profound truth.

Through one-on-one consultations, public talks, daily social media postings, writing collaborations, online groups, and events, Janine is here in her passion, igniting the spark in every heart, ready to open into truth.

Contact with Janine:

Website: https://www.theheartlady.net/

Facebook: https://www.facebook.com/janine.savient.9/

LinkedIn: https://www.linkedin.com/in/janinesavient/

Instagram: https://www.instagram.com/janine.savient/

Email: janine.savient@gmail.com

CHAPTER 10

Embracing Your Heart's Wisdom

A JOURNEY TO ABUNDANCE AND SERENITY

Gwenda Smith, Spirit Medicine Woman, Wellness Mentor

MY STORY

Every day that I came on shift, she seemed to fade away a little more. Her eyes held no light anymore, the spark of cheekiness that was once so beautiful to see, the dance in her eyes when she looked at him. All of it was gone.

A few days later, I came on shift, and she was gone, the bed empty, and the room cold. I cried as I thought of this dear lady who died of a broken heart.

A few months before, her husband and only love had passed from this world. This couple inspired me.

The way they looked at each other and cuddled was full of love and care. There was a light in their eyes that I hadn't seen before in an elderly couple. The keen interest each one showed toward the other when they spoke was as if they were in an early stage of their relationship.

All my years of nursing did not shield my heart from the sorrow I felt as I watched her fade away after her husband passed from this world.

This beautiful couple had been together for over 60 years. They were in a room together at the home, and that would be their last. It wasn't the home they had known together, the one that held their memories of a family and was laced with special couches and ornaments on the sideboards.

I smiled as I thought of the loving stories they both shared with me about the family visits—the aroma of the roast lunches that greeted the family as they arrived, and how the house was alive with the laughter and love of the family when they got together.

That house was home to five generations of their family. It held many memories of daily life and the celebration of a life beginning and a life ending.

Sharing a small glass of brandy by the log fire at the end of a long, cold day was a special time this couple enjoyed throughout their marriage.

I felt the love in their words whenever they shared a story with me. But now that he was gone, she was brokenhearted; her eyes had lost that amazing sparkle.

My time with this couple was an important part of my puzzle in learning to know the wisdom of my heart and the eternal wellspring of love in it.

When I began my quest to understand disease, illness, and dying, I took many courses, looking for answers to the mystery. One of the topics I learned about is the energy field of the human body and the layers of that field of energy that surround the physical body.

Did you know that the energy field of the heart is the largest of our subtle bodies? If you were to be sitting across the room from me at the cardiologist's waiting room, my heart energy would reach yours. The energy being carried in my field would become interwoven with yours.

This powerful energy can affect the vibration of your field, so much so that it can affect the reading of your blood pressure. This is why we can feel the pain of loss someone is experiencing.

During my years of nursing, I witnessed the loss of life because of a broken heart many times. When my father passed from this world, I thought my heart would never be the same again, and that I wouldn't be able to love again.

How could it be that my love for my father created a belief that I wouldn't be able to love again? My father believed in me. He would tell me that I could do anything I put my mind to. He never doubted my dreams. He was the one person who believed in me. When he left this world, I felt that a piece of my heart had left, too. It was only in the years of teaching myself to know my heart and embrace the wellspring of eternal, pure love and joy held in every heart that I learned how to be in union with my heart.

When I was in my 20s, I thought I knew what my heart wanted, what love was all about, and what being loved felt like. How wrong I was!

When I was about 34, I thought I found the love of my life, the one and only. The day came, and we married. As I glided around the dance floor with my dad in my gone-with-the-wind style wedding gown, I stepped on Dad's foot. He smiled. Luckily, it was my wedding night. Dad was never impressed when his dance partner stood on his foot.

He asked me, "Are you happy, luv?" I smiled back and beamed the biggest smile as I said, "Oh, yes, Dad, I am. I found the one. And I am older and wiser."

He smiled back at me and said, "Remember, you can be all that you want to be, and most of all, be happy in yourself."

WE ARE ALL DIFFERENT IN THE WAY THAT WE WANT TO BE LOVED AND WHAT IT MEANS TO US.

Have you had a pet in your life that was better than your best friend?

I've had two Rottweilers, each with distinct personalities. The first was Caesar and the second was Suvius.

Caesar could speak. He would say, "Hello Mum." It delighted me so much to see the look on friends' faces when they heard him. They would exclaim, "Is he talking?"

He passed from non-Hodgkin's lymphoma, the same disease my father had.

Suvius was an amazing companion. He came to work with me every day and night at the health centre. The clients loved him, and he them. On a cold, wet winter's night, he collapsed and passed tragically. My heart was torn apart. I cannot express in words the intensity of grief. I felt lost and alone, and I wanted to die.

I used to drive to a Vietnamese Buddha garden and sit praying for help for the pain in my heart. One day, while sobbing heavily at the feet of the huge statue of Quan Yin, my heart was in so much pain I prayed for help.

A warmth came over me, and a gentle voice said: *Know your heart; heal your pain.*

I sobbed all the way home. When I came inside the house I went and sat in my healing room and prayed for help and guidance. This began my journey of introspection and learning to know my heart. The greatest gift you can give yourself is time to listen to your heart's wisdom, feel what your heart is holding, and give yourself love. This is knowing the wisdom of your heart.

To know how I wanted to be loved and what love meant to me, I had to make a determined commitment to myself. I needed to learn more about who I was as opposed to who I had become to be loved, accepted, and thought of in the way family and friends wanted to think of me. That was an astounding revelation.

I made that revelation when I looked back at my relationship with the two most important people in my life, my dad and my gran. I loved my mum and other family members, too. But I had a special bond with Dad and his mum.

It was at that time I realised they loved the person they wanted me to be.

I became the master of observing myself and learned more about my feelings and reactions, as well as my sense of being accepted and fitting in.

I began to pay attention to the way my body felt when I had a strong feeling come over me. This newfound mastery was life-changing. I share this practice with clients. It's wonderful to see how their hearts change when they discover the infinite, eternal love we all hold within our hearts.

Taking that journey helped me know what love truly is and what it means to be loved. I found the most serene peace and calm can be called upon at any moment of distress or anguish. Even anger can be stilled and transformed when we're in union with the wisdom of our hearts.

One certainty is this: until we truly know what love means and what it is to be loved, we'll struggle to have true love, peace, and serenity in our hearts.

If you and I were sitting together and I asked you to tell me what love means to you, what would you say? Most often, people tell me all about the person they love, going into detail about how wonderful the person is.

But the question is, can you tell me what love means to you? Can you see the difference?

When we know what love means to us, we can be guided by the magic of the wisdom in our hearts.

The next thing I would ask you is: What does it mean to be loved? Typically, I get a very similar answer to the first question, where the focus is all about the other person, the cat, the dog, or sometimes a bird!

Why would I ask what it means to be loved? Our perception of love stems from our upbringing and observing the relationships of our parents or partners. This is a false perception that leads to false beliefs about ourselves and love. It usually leads us down a path of many heartaches and heartbreaks, even into abusive relationships.

The power you can find by knowing what it means to be loved is amazing. Remember, I mentioned that after the loss of my father, I didn't think I'd trust love again. This was a false perception of what it is to be loved. I didn't know what love meant to me. I couldn't be in union with the wisdom of my heart.

WHAT IT MEANS TO EMBRACE THE WISDOM OF YOUR HEART

To know what love means to you and how you want to be loved is an essential key to knowing the wisdom of your heart. Earlier I mentioned that the energy field of the heart can reach across a room; to be precise the subtle energy field of the heart is powerful beyond measure. This subtle field meets anyone within 15 feet (4.572 meters) of your physical body.

This energy vibrates at the high frequency of pure love and joy. However, if you are carrying old wounds related to a love gone sour, such as jealousy, insecurity, anxiety, abandonment, sorrow, or grief, the energy field is hampered by the lower vibrations of these emotions.

A heart weighed down with hurt, despair, and grief can't be open, which means we struggle to find a love that makes us happy and to feel at ease and peace in all aspects of our lives. We can find that we're always looking for something, chasing dreams, and losing dreams.

The wisdom the heart holds is magical, amazing, and powerful. To know the wisdom of your heart means you can heal from life's challenges with more ease. You become deeply peaceful and find that there is a soul-fuelled solution to any situation or hurt that comes along the path of life.

To embrace the wisdom of the heart means that abundance in all that life offers is more easily attained. To be fit, well, healthy, strong, and vital are important aspects of true abundance. Though often, abundance is thought of as wealth in status, assets, and money.

This is the abundance the ego seeks and is far removed from the wisdom of the heart. When we're in union with the wisdom of our heart, we're in union with the frequency of pure love and joy. Our physical body is agile, strong, healthy, and full of vitality. Our mind is free of cluttered, scattered thoughts of worry, overwhelm, fear, and anxiousness.

To strive for the abundance of wealth in assets, money, and status can bring stress, illness, and loss of sense of oneself, and alignment with the soul and the Almighty Divine, which to me is God. You may have a different reference for the creator of all that is.

No one would pass from this world of a broken heart or heart disease if all hearts were united in the magic of wisdom and love.

Love is the key to knowing the wisdom of the heart; love is the magic of the wisdom. Embracing the wisdom of your heart is the way to a life that is rich and abundant in all aspects. I'd like to gift you with simple practices you can do to take that journey of knowing your heart and embracing a deep, serene peace and calm.

THE PRACTICE

1. **Quiet Contemplation:** Make time every day to be in a space that brings you a sense of harmony and happiness. As you sit quietly imagine you're opening a door, a golden door at the front of your heart. Ask your heart to flow a golden stream of pure joy through

your body. Breathe deeply and slowly let yourself imagine that golden stream flowing through your body.

2. **An offering:** Every night, as you settle into sleep, breathe into your heart and fill your chest with gentleness and compassion. Letting go of all that is less than kindness and gentleness towards yourself.

3. **Clear your mind:** Before beginning and ending the day, clear your mind of all that is less than love and joy. Let all worries and stress be left behind. This practice allows your heart to be open and expansive.

4. **Make a promise:** Begin every morning with a promise to your heart that you will listen and follow its gentle whispers of wisdom.

5. **Gratitude:** The practice of daily gratitude is a must for a life that is enriched and abundant in all that you wish for. Say aloud the things that you are grateful for every day. The reason we say it aloud is that our words carry a higher frequency when spoken and even more when we weave them with love and joy.

6. **Body mapping:** Make time every day to tune into your body. The hurts and wounds we carry can spill over from the heart to other parts of the body. For example, shoulder problems, a frozen shoulder, and chest infections are a spillover from a hurt or wound that has burdened the heart for too long. When you use body mapping you can release the blocked energy and heal your heart and body.

7. **Be gracious:** In all that you do all that you say and think, carry graciousness, for this is the way of the soul and heart. There are times that the experiences we have bring pain upset, anger, and even resentment. Be quick to recognise these emotions, let them go and fill your energy with graciousness.

8. **Observe:** Observe your thoughts and decide if they're uplifting, inspiring, kind, and helpful to yourself and others. If not, pause and observe the conversation or situation, and then decide what you want to feel. Act accordingly.

9. **Love:** Embrace loving yourself deeply and freely. A heart that is full of love overflows and has a radiance that brings love to all whom it touches.

10. **Acceptance:** Accept your mistakes, decisions, and choices without judgment. Give loving forgiveness for anything you speak harshly about to yourself or to others.

Gwenda Smith is a spirit medicine woman, a leader in integrated wellness and spiritual mentorship.

A driven, dedicated Spiritual mentor, taking students on a pathway of ascension and transformation.

A dynamic, warm, inspiring, and powerful internationally recognized speaker.

Her vision is to show you the way to your inner greatness and innate wisdom so that you can be free to live every day knowing how to release pain, illness, and disease. To live life on your terms, the way your soul came to experience this world.

When Gwenda is relaxing, she can be found with her nose in a good book with a glass of fine French champagne or at the gym. Two extremes, you might say. But that is her, never the ordinary. Never the usual ho-hum way for her.

She loves to have fun and enjoy time with friends and family, usually with some great tunes to dance to and upbeat conversations.

A trial blazer from the day she arrived in this world, she has always seen rules as constricting on her heart and soul.

Connect with Gwenda:

Website: https://www.healwithgwenda.com

Facebook: https://www.facebook.com/healwithgwenda

Instagram: https://www.instagram.com/healwithgwenda_health_wellness

LinkedIn: https://www.linkedin.com/in/healwithgwendagwendasmith/

CHAPTER 11

Throw Some Love at It!

EMBRACING VULNERABILITY ON THE PUBLIC STAGE

Susan Ernst

MY STORY

The word *yacht* was my undoing. In the third-grade spotlight, with the class's eyes fixed on me, I faltered, turning a simple vocabulary exercise into an indelible lesson in humiliation.

The classroom vocabulary exercise was a rite of passage. One by one, we faced the class, armed only with our budding egos, as our teacher scrawled the word on the chalkboard. When it was your turn, your job was to pronounce the word and use it in a sentence. I loved vocabulary! I always got A's! I stepped up, bursting with confidence, yet unaware of the trap set before me. The word was *yacht*. "YACKET" I declared proudly, only to be met with a wave of raucous laughter.

That unleashed laughter was like a tidal wave sweeping away my confidence and leaving me stranded in a sea of embarrassment. I remember the heat that flooded my cheeks, my hands trembling at my sides, and the floor swaying beneath my feet. I stood there with a stupid grin on my face, trying to become invisible as the teacher struggled to settle the class.

I returned to my seat, my classmates' laughter still ringing in my ears. I felt a seed of vulnerability take root within me. Over time, it grew in the shadows of my self-doubt, fueled by the memory of that day. The word *yacht* became more than a vocabulary challenge. It marked the birth of my lifelong struggle with public speaking.

Years passed, and with them came new stages and new audiences. Each time I approached the podium, subconsciously, the ghost of 'YACKET' hovered at the edge of my consciousness, a reminder of the vulnerability exposed in the bright light of a third-grade classroom.

The journey to overcome that moment has been long and rocky. There have been triumphs, certainly, moments when my voice carried with strength and clarity. But there have also been stumbles, times when the laughter seemed to echo from the past, threatening to unravel the progress I made. In fact, it wasn't until very recently that this memory resurfaced, and I faced the humiliation I felt so long ago. This recognition and a significant realization changed how I greet a public speaking opportunity.

Picture Them in Their Underwear!

As I stepped up to the lectern, the church was filled with a serene silence, punctuated only by the soft rustling of pages as the congregation searched their bulletins. The stained-glass window above the altar cast a kaleidoscope of colors across the pews as the congregation waited for me to speak.

Take a deep, slow breath. One. Two. Three. Four. Can they see what I'm doing? Exhale slowly. One. Two. Three. Four. Smile, for Pete's sake! Relax your stomach muscles. Bend your knees. Not that much! Good grief. Find a friend in that humungous sea of people looking up at you. Picture them in their underwear!

I began to read the scripture, my voice steady and clear. Those words of wisdom and truth—the words I so loved to share with others—flowed from my heart, filling that sacred space with their message. I felt a swell of emotion, perhaps joy and relief rolled into one, as I delivered the final verse. "The word of God for the people of God. Amen."

And there it was again. Like clockwork! A sudden light-headedness overcame me. The room began to spin, and the vibrant colors of the windows blurred into a whirlwind of hues. The congregation looked like they were sitting behind a current of slow-moving water. Their smiles of approval faded into a grey fog as my neck muscles clenched and pain smacked me between the eyes. I stepped down from the altar and walked the length of the sanctuary, as if in quicksand, to the Narthex just beyond.

I woke to hear voices above me. "I think she's having an aneurysm! I saw it on TV once. We better call 911!"

I am not having an aneurysm!

I tried to scream, but no words could get past my clenched jaw. I realized at that moment that I was lying face up on the cold tile floor of the Narthex surrounded by worried faces, all blurred while my eyes squinted against the vice grip of a migraine taking hold. *I must have fainted.*

As the whispers of concern and the gentle touch of hands brought me back to the present, a pang of recognition twisted in my heart. This wasn't the first time the joy of reading scripture was overshadowed by the sudden onset of debilitating pain. Once again, I internalized my fear so much that no one knew anything was wrong—until it was.

Lying there with someone's folded coat now cushioning my head, I remembered the last time I read scripture in front of the congregation. The same overwhelming sense of fulfillment was quickly followed by a familiar, throbbing ache that crept across my temples and held me in its vice for three relentless days.

It seemed ironic that sharing my love for the divine word could take such a toll on me. The migraines were like thieves stealing the warmth of the light I felt in those moments of connection with my faith and community.

Pause. Take a breath.

Why does the spotlight unnerve me so? Each time I faced an audience, it was like standing at the edge of a tall cliff, my voice threatening to plummet into the abyss below. The fear was tangible, a shroud that wrapped around me, suffocating my good intentions.

Yet, I didn't give up. There was a flicker of something else—a spark of defiance, a whisper of courage that kept pushing me to try again. *Come on! You can do this! You are better than this!* It was a flame that fear could not extinguish, no matter how hard it tried.

In that moment, I made a silent vow: *I will not let my fear define me. I will figure out where this fear is coming from and defeat it.*

Fast-forward to the present:

Everyone here loves you! There is no reason to be nervous! Get over it!

Having recently relocated from California to Maryland, I joined a women's networking group—the On Purpose Woman Global Community—to grow my commercial real estate appraisal business. A few months ago, the group's founder invited me to take a five-minute spot in front of the group. She supports women with opportunities for deep connection, more visibility, and being comfortable playing a more significant role on the planet. It was an opportunity to tell them a bit about me and share what I'm passionate about. The day's theme was "Thriving Together: Creating Possibilities Through Connection."

As I stood up to speak, I looked around the room, and all I saw were heart-centered women, each wrapped up in loving-kindness. It was palpable. *No reason to be nervous! B R E A T H E!*

"Thank you, Ginny, for this exciting opportunity! What perfect timing! I want to share a story with you: a story about thriving. Thriving after a move across the country. Thriving after a redesign of my business and celebrating what has come from new connections!

I founded my business over 30 years ago. But I want to tell you about my side hustle! I write children's stories!"

Don't focus on the audience! Focus on your speech!

"My inspiration for writing children's stories came from volunteer work in Cambodia. For five years, I joined a team of close friends from several churches in the US and volunteered at a rescue center just outside of Phenom Penh. We served about 100 kids each day who had been rescued from, or were at risk of, sex trafficking. We played games, sang songs, listened to stories, and made crafts. Striving to bless each child, we were doubly blessed. This work was life-changing."

Your knees are locked. Bend your knees!

"The kids ranged in age from about four to about fifteen. I fell in love with each of those precious kids and vowed that I would find a way to help that rescue center in their amazing fight against sex trafficking."

Don't cry! Get a grip!

"Many rescued children come from families who live and work at the nearby brick factories. The families are nothing more than indentured servants. They make bricks from the clay earth surrounding the factories and bake them in huge kilns. In exchange, they are allowed to live in makeshift shacks that are not much more than a lean-to made of a few pieces of tin and cardboard. Many of these families cannot survive, and this is one place where desperate parents will sell their child into the sex trade."

* * *

My talk was greeted with energized applause, and I tried as I might to steady my heartbeat. I hid my clenched jaw behind a stiff smile. I clasped my hands in my lap to stop the shaking. That now familiar headache was slowly marching up the back of my neck. Thankfully, my friend Jennifer was scheduled to speak next, and the attention was moving to her.

As I drove home that day, I wondered for the thousandth time why I became so nervous. *What am I afraid of? Will I ever get this under control?*

Throw some love at it!

Jennifer and I agreed to check in on Zoom the next morning. She answered the phone after one ring. "So, you were great yesterday! I enjoyed your talk very much!" I said, settling in for what I knew would be an enjoyable chat.

"Oh, so were you, Sue! You did a great job!"

"Oh, please, how can you say that Jenn? I started blubbering right in the middle of the whole thing! And I was shaking! It was a hot mess!" I laughed nervously.

"Did you see how several of the women started crying when they saw you crying? (I hadn't. Deer in the headlights.) Did you see how they nodded in affirmation when you spoke of the importance of teaching kids how to be brave? (No.) It was palpable."

Jennifer sat quietly for a moment.

"Why do I do that? Why can't I get through a talk without falling apart? I love talking about the kids in Cambodia. I adore those kids, and I love telling others about them! I do the same thing at church when asked to read scripture. I love doing that!"

Jennifer looked at me nonchalantly, raised her hand, shook her head slightly as if to imply this was a no-brainer, and said, "Just throw some love at it!"

I stared at the computer screen, and she returned the stare with a smile.

"Now I know what gets you in trouble when speaking in front of others! It's not the act of speaking. You're great. You're feeling vulnerable, and you're embarrassed to show your vulnerabilities. It's okay! Your vulnerability is what makes people love you!"

That was a breakthrough moment for me. It was clear to me then. Yes, of course, the people in church care about me as I care about them. And the attendees at the networking meeting were curious about what I had to tell them. That was not the issue. I understood that when Jennifer said, "Throw some love at it!" she meant, "Throw some love at yourself! Be kind to yourself."

I realized that once I learned to love myself and accept myself, vulnerabilities and all, I could feel comfortable in my own skin and genuinely follow my passions without worrying about how that looks.

THE PRACTICE

If you're a loving person, you'll attract others who love you. But that's missing the point. You must love yourself first. Love is the antidote to fear. Embrace your flaws and vulnerabilities. They are what makes your voice unique.

Believing in yourself is an act of self-love. It also means owning your shadows. Brené Brown says in her book *Daring Greatly*, "Only when we are brave enough to explore the darkness will we discover the infinite power of our light."

When you believe in yourself, you go out and chase your dreams. It turns your inner critic into your best friend and your cheerleader.

I'm practicing self-love at this late stage in my life. Loving yourself is not always easy, but it's essential for your well-being and happiness. You're more confident, resilient, and compassionate when you love yourself.

During my deep dive into self-love, I realized it's essential for many reasons.

When you love yourself:

- It improves your mental and emotional health.
- You will have higher self-esteem.

- You will take care of your body.
- You will seek new skills and seek new opportunities.
- You will attract and maintain healthy and fulfilling relationships.

Here are four steps you can take to start loving yourself more:

1. **Practice self-acceptance.** Self-acceptance means embracing yourself as you are without judging or rejecting any aspect of your being. Self-acceptance helps you appreciate your uniqueness and diversity and respect your choices and decisions.

2. **Practice self-compassion.** Self-compassion means treating yourself with kindness, understanding, and forgiveness, especially when suffering, struggling, or failing. It means recognizing that you're human, imperfect, and share a common humanity with others who face challenges and difficulties.

3. **Practice self-care.** Self-care means caring for your physical, mental, emotional, and spiritual well-being. It also means engaging in activities that nourish your mind, heart, and soul, such as hobbies, passions, learning, meditation, prayer, or volunteering. Self-care helps you maintain your health, happiness, and balance and prevent burnout and exhaustion.

4. **Practice self-expression.** Self-expression means expressing your authentic voice and creative potential. It means communicating your thoughts, feelings, opinions and desires with confidence. It means pursuing your goals, dreams, and passions in a way that aligns with your values and purpose. Authentic self-expression will honor your identity, fulfill your potential, and contribute to the world.

I love what Pema Chodron says about self-love in her book *The Wisdom of No Escape: And the Path of Loving-Kindness.*

"But loving-kindness – maitri – toward ourselves doesn't mean getting rid of anything. Maitri means that we can still be crazy after all these years. We can still be angry after all these years. We can still be timid, jealous, or full of feelings of unworthiness. The point is not to try to change ourselves. Meditation practice isn't about trying to throw ourselves away and become something better. It's about befriending who we are already. The ground of practice is you, me, or whoever we are right now, just as we are. That's the ground, that's what we study; that's what we come to know with tremendous curiosity and interest."

Love is not just a feeling; It's a force that transforms fear into courage and silence into song. I find my voice in the quiet moments when I listen to my heart. May your voice be heard, and love guide you through every fear.

Susan Ernst is a passionate bestselling children's book author and expert commercial real estate appraiser. She started her appraisal business in 1990 and now focuses on reviewing appraisals for her commercial lending clients.

Susan grew up in Mill Valley, California, and lived on the West Coast until recently moving to Chevy Chase, Maryland, to live near family. She has two beautiful daughters, Laura and Alissa, and is a happy grandmother of two.

Volunteer work in Cambodia inspired her to write children's stories. For five years, Susan accompanied heart-centered volunteers serving children at a rescue center led by Agape International Missions (AIM) located in Svay Pak, Cambodia. This nonprofit organization works to rescue, heal, and empower survivors of trafficking. After witnessing the heartbreaking work accomplished at AIM, she vowed to help those children have hope and be brave!

You can read Susan's first children's story in *Brave Kids, Short Stories to Inspire Our Future World Changers, Volume 1, Chapter 20: Chann is Called to the Principal's Office. A Change of Heart Can Help!* Her second story is in *Brave Kids Volume 2, Chapter 2: Jasmine Saves the Day! Trusting Your Instincts.* Look for *Brave Kids Volume 3* in 2025! **Proceeds from sales of her books go to AIM.**

Susan gratefully joined her skilled co-author team to share her story in *Gifts of Wisdom—Practices for Healing and Empowerment* for what she considers a "gift for all generations."

Connect with Susan:

Website: https://www.sueernst.com

Facebook: https://www.facebook.com/sernst992/

LinkedIn: https://www.linkedin.com/in/susan-ernst-57b87272/

CHAPTER 12

Relationship Power

WISDOM FOR CREATING A LONGER, HEALTHIER, AND HAPPIER LIFE

Ilene L. Dillon, MSW, LMFT, LCSW

MY STORY

The phone rang. 2:30 am. *It's that damn obscene phone caller.* **Why** *does he keep calling?* Fumbling for my flashlight, I went to the phone on the kitchen wall, carefully avoiding furniture recently placed in my still-new-to-me home.

He only says "hello," then breathes before he hangs up. I didn't know what to do. Calls started three days after my husband walked out. *It's gotta be a neighbor who heard us arguing and could see lights going on and off,* I reasoned. I was terrified, living alone for the first time in my life.

"Why?" I wailed into the phone, stomping my feet in frustration. I banged the receiver back onto its cradle, returned to bed, and stared into the blackness above me. *As long as I stay awake, I cannot be taken by surprise.* My mind raced; my body shuddered. *My toddler and I could be attacked as we slept.* Finally, I fell into a fitful sleep.

Night after night.

Growing up was awful for me, with neglect, serious injury and illness, institutional living, and permanent removal from my birth mother at age two. There was more. Constant relocation with my military family—never seeing school friends again. I didn't know how to focus on positive possibilities.

In college, I met my future husband. Our families were dysfunctional. We married at age 19. With him, I felt loved, that I mattered, and almost normal. We moved to the opposite coast, renting a small houseboat in the middle of Seattle, Washington. We made a pact to help each other complete undergraduate and master's degrees. Eight years into the marriage, adding a baby unexpectedly destroyed our relationship.

It's daytime. Why is the phone ringing so loudly? Struggling out of bed, my estranged husband's voice sounded friendly. He was already living with another woman, yet confusingly, he frequently called to confess, "I love you."

If you love me, why aren't you here to protect us? I felt both safer and confused. "That man called again last night. I couldn't get him to talk to me. He never answered when I said 'hello.'"

Sounding alarmed, my husband challenged, "You talked to him? *Never* talk to obscene callers. No wonder he keeps calling. Just hang up!"

"I didn't know," I said, feeling weak and stupid. Growing up, I was restricted from using the phone. Now I was an adult with a house and a baby. I was finishing my master's degree and becoming a psychotherapist to help others. Yet I didn't know I should not speak to obscene callers. *How will I make it?*

2:45 a.m. The phone rang again. I didn't answer. *He knows I'm here.* I panicked. *What if he breaks in and stabs me and my daughter?* Shaking, I was unable to stop thinking about the violence. Abruptly, the ringing stopped. *I hate this!*

I need help from someone more powerful than me. I talked aloud to God.

"Okay God, truth be told, I don't want to die at all. People say death is inevitable. I'll accept it if I have to, but I don't want me or my daughter to die a violent death. You're God. You're omnipotent. You have to keep us safe. I can't do this by myself. I also don't want to worry for my whole life. I'm turning this over to you. Please take care of us." I added a "Thank you." I didn't want to sound too demanding.

Returning to bed, I crawled under the covers and fell into a peaceful sleep. The obscene phone caller dialed my number only one more time, ever. I learned not to respond to him. I know now that when we learn a *lesson* that has been presented to us through our experience, that *lesson* is over. I'm a believer. Never another obscene phone call in 52 years.

I had other lessons and much more to learn. I didn't know how to do many of the jobs in my suddenly-different life. I had to make decisions and take full responsibility for two lives. I was financially dependent on a man who reneged on his agreement to parent with me. *How will I find the time and resources to finish my last year of graduate school, alone with a year-old child?*

"We have an agreement," I reminded my husband. "You need to support us financially through this year. Then I'll be able to earn an income and take care of us, which will be better for you. Here's how much I'll need. Promise me you'll do this." Wisely, he agreed. I still had to find childcare and time to study.

I didn't share my deep pain. *I've been abandoned—again. The story of my life. I knew this was going to happen. I never wanted things to be this way. I did everything I could to make things work. I hate this. What's wrong with me? No matter what, I will not let my child be miserable like I was.*

My brain exploded. *Nobody cares about me or my daughter. I never thought I would be alone with all of this. Now it's all up to me. Why did he do this to me?*

I was always told what to do and punished if I didn't do it. My parents made life-changing decisions without consulting me. I'd always been powerless. Now, for the first time, I directed my own life. Nobody else was there. Scary—like a nightmare. Things shifted. Figuring things out was *all up to me.*

I needed to figure out how to parent—alone. *I have to make decisions and a plan. I don't want to parent like my parents parented me. How do you parent alone? How will I know I'm making the right decisions? And what about this awful anger pouring out of me? Where do I begin?*

I could not quit or fold. My daughter needed me. Somehow, I had to immediately transform into a powerful, effective person who made good adult decisions.

I surprised myself with my success over the next ten years of hard work. In graduate school, I made all As. I developed a parenting method (Conscious Parenting) that emphasized decision-making and character development and was based on spiritual principles. My daughter developed self-confidence, responsibility, and creativity and made thoughtful decisions. I made money teaching this method to families and schools in the US and abroad. *Lemonade from lemons.*

Still, I desperately needed to know more about anger: Why do we have it? What's it for? What is it? And how do I deal with it? Constantly seeking, my search took years. We cannot get rid of emotions (they're energy), but we can *master emotions.* Anger can be transformed into *enthusiasm.*

At first, there were no answers to my questions. Eventually, I made discoveries and tried them out in my own life. When something worked, I offered it to my therapy clients, who were eager to experiment. We all felt better. Our lives improved. When the Covid epidemic occurred, former clients (sometimes from 40 years before) asked me for "checkups."

The work we did with emotions was still intact. What they learned about emotions still worked well for them. I realized I discovered a totally unique and powerful way of understanding and working with emotions. No one I spoke to viewed emotions the same way. What I discovered was practical, effective, and lasting. Plus, it was *simple.*

I had advanced from "Very Angry Person," to "Recovering Angry Person," to "Recovered Angry Person," which I am today. Eventually, I learned to *partner with anger,* using anger as it's designed to work for us.

I published my first book, *Emotions in Motion: Mastering Life's Built-in Navigation System.* I also wrote about *Realigning with Anger* and *Outgrowing Manipulation.* I became a professional speaker, Amazon bestselling author, and master teacher with a 13-year podcast, *Full Power Living,* focused on "awakening the world to the power and importance of human emotions."

1994—I made my most life-altering decision and life change. While researching *Exploring Love with Your Child* (a book for teaching parents how to help their children with emotions), one resource proclaimed:

"Love is Love, is Love. It doesn't matter whether you love yourself or you love someone else. *What does matter is that you choose to live by love,* to embody the principle of love."

I chose love, and everything changed.

We've all been taught many things that don't work. Prevalent is the notion of living from the "outside, in." Disney's famous song promises, "Someday, my prince will come." A great thought but pure fantasy. We believe we must *find* love.

Human life has been created to work best from the "inside out." We need to *become* the loving prince we seek. Once we have what we believe we *need*, it manifests in our lives. The love we hold inside attracts others to us. They *mirror* the love we already have.

That author's words made sense to me. I chose to become and live by love. My life transformed and changed forever. What a radical concept:

We need to love ourselves, first and foremost, to have the love we want!

For years, I believed I was not lovable. By loving myself first, I no longer needed someone to love me. Self-love was not selfish. I felt loved all the time—no deficit. What if *everyone* is lovable? I realized loving myself brings love to me; then, I share love with the world.

Learning to love myself was arduous and took time. When I started using the advice I received, I could barely do it. I decided to stop judging myself. I learned the power of living by principles. And I kept asking myself, *How will I behave when I truly love myself?* With determination, consciousness, and effort, I did it!

The more I loved myself—and could feel it—the more I understood the idea that life is designed to be lived from the *inside out.* Changing *only me* brought amazing, profound changes into every part of my life. Even strangers now treated me with thoughtfulness, kindness, and even love. What a radical departure from my earlier life.

Learning to love myself is the most important thing I have ever done for myself or my family. All our lives were transformed when there was plenty of love. And it all started inside of me.

My life transformed. After 20 years as a single parent, I remarried. My husband was a respected and successful neurosurgeon who loved me, invited me to watch him do brain surgery (I loved it), and upgraded my life. To function well with him (a man accustomed to wielding power and being "top of the heap"), I developed a core of personal power in myself.

With him, I experienced more support than ever before for my work, my choices, and for being my full self. Together, we gave speeches and published writings. He pointedly helped me improve the organization of my brain. In turn, I shared with him how to work powerfully with emotions. Ours was a wonderful relationship and collaboration.

Just over 20 years together, my husband died of cancer at home, with his family gathered around and loving him, just as he wanted. He welcomed the release from pain, and I lost my fear of death.

More new chapters opened in my life.

I cleared out and sold our house, bought an RV, and became a full-time RVer, roaming North America with my little dog, Pi. We've had wonderful, loving experiences, demonstrating again that the love I have inside of me *is reflected to me* from the outside.

I've been writing, speaking for conferences, appearing on podcasts and summits, coaching and being a therapist, and sharing with the world the amazing things I've learned about emotions. Partnering with anger protects us from mental and physical illness, enhances self-esteem, and lifts depression.

I now know that life here on Earth is designed for our transformative learning. As we *Realign with Emotions*, we learn the profound yet simple system offered for our learning. Engaging with this system facilitates our positive transformation. We can do this work ourselves and enjoy flow, ease, and joy.

You and me—all of us—are students in the giant school called Earth.

Our primary support and challenge is exploring love. Choosing love!

Live the life you want to lead. Love yourself first, and experience love spreading and then being reflected back to you.

THE PRACTICE

In 2023 CNBC reported findings from a research study started by Harvard Researchers in 1938. This 85-year-long study investigated what makes people happy.

724 male participants shared health records, answered detailed personal questions, and their family members were interviewed. Teenagers at the beginning, study participants were men of various economic and social backgrounds, from the poorest to Harvard undergrads. President John F. Kennedy was an original participant. Approximately 60 original participants are still participating.

The results? Positive relationships consistently correlated with a happy life. Study subjects were happier, healthier, and lived longer when they had positive relationships.

Google says:

A positive relationship should bring more happiness than unhappiness

They're characterized by:

- **Honesty:** Partners are honest with each other, including emotionally.

- **Respect:** Partners accept differences, seeing each other *as they are*.

- **Trust:** Partners are trustable and trust each other.

- **Notice the positives:** Partners share appreciation for positive qualities.

- **Communication:** Partners maintain connection through communication.

- **Empathy:** Partners feel *with* each other rather than *for* each other.

- **Forgiveness:** Partners value the relationship highest of all, releasing hurts.

For 53 of the 85-year Harvard study, I've worked as a marriage and family counselor and psychotherapist. My clients and I have worked to release "problems" and develop positive relationships.

Most people are challenged to develop the positive relationships needed for happiness. Why? Because we haven't developed a positive relationship with ourselves. Creating positive relationships with others occurs naturally and easily when we feel loved.

Unfortunately, most of us have been taught to live our lives from the outside in, not from the inside out.

If someone wants a loving partner, they're encouraged to *find* someone to love them. That's living life from *outside in*. Sometimes it works, but it's not reliable because of this principle:

What you have inside of you, you tend to attract from outside of you

When we "hunt for love," we pay attention to the problem: love is missing. Living as an *outside in* person, we place attention on what we don't have. Paying attention to this problem feeds it energy. It grows. Searching *out there* to find someone to give us the love we believe we must get from others can make our problem worse.

Ironically, we end up attracting someone who also believes, "I don't have the love I need." They're hoping we bring them their *missing love.* Two people who are expecting another to provide them with what they're missing. Think of your own relationship experiences. How does this combined neediness work?

Contrast this with the "fill myself with love first" system. We build love inside us, ending love deprivation. We've got so much love it spills over onto others. We're no longer needy, seeking someone to fill us with love. Instead, love inside of us is mirrored back to us, abundantly.

Life is an inside-out design. Loving ourselves first makes us a love generator, adding to and spreading love for the whole world. It's not selfish. Filled with love, we feel it, share it, and spread it. Whether alone or with others, we're filled with love.

We're now in a *foundational positive relationship*, experiencing more happiness than unhappiness—with ourselves and with others, too. We're focused continually on feeling good and living joyfully.

We *attract love* when the love we already have inside is reflected from the outside. By creating love internally, we've *become* love. People entering our lives bring *their excess love* to us because *like attracts like.* They're filled with love, too. We can't lose. Creating the love we want inside of us fills us with love *and* brings love to us.

I didn't know how to love myself. I asked for help. Here is the simple method:

> Sit quietly, eyes closed. In your mind's eye, envision a baby—animal or human. Feel your love for that baby. Now, transfer that feeling of love from the baby to yourself.

At first, I could maintain that feeling for five seconds. I kept at it. Eventually, I could love myself for longer. Then, *loving me became a part of me.*

I was in a lasting positive relationship with myself. I practiced the same positive relationships behaviors, this time with myself.

- **Honesty:** I'm honest with myself, especially regarding what I feel.

- **Respect:** I accept myself as I am, changing only if I want to. I know we all have strengths and flaws. I accept mine.

- **Trust:** I experience myself as the amazing person I am, worthy of trust, self-belief, and loving support.

- **Notice the positives:** I'm grateful for who I am and my good character, able to notice, appreciate, and share my positive qualities.

- **Communication:** I enjoy communicating with myself. The spoken word has power. Conversing aloud helps me understand and sort things out.

- **Empathy:** I'm kinder to myself. I realize I'm human. I do the best I can with what I know at the time.

- **Forgiveness:** Forgiveness means to let go. I let go of self-judgment, self-blame, and negative self-talk. I love myself as unconditionally as I can.

When you stop judging yourself, you stop judging others, too. And they stop judging you. The way to end judgment in your life is to end it inside of you.

We all want to be happy.

Harvard investigators have revealed that throughout our lives, people who report being happiest have had positive relationships.

The fastest, most reliable, and most complete way to develop *positive relationships* in your life is to live *inside out*, establishing your foundational positive relationship with yourself.

Start now!

Ilene Dillon gave up on her search to be "normal" back in the 1990s. She always wanted to fit in. It turned out the only one she could really "fit in" with was herself!

Ilene loves relating intensely. She's not afraid to ask the hard questions, push for answers regarding life's challenges and mysteries, or take risks. She once swam in the ocean with a full-grown cougar.

A psychotherapist and marriage/family counselor for a half-century, Ilene is also an international keynote speaker and originated and hosted her podcast, "Full Power Living," for 13 years. She's a master instructor for Parenting Consciously, Realigning with Anger and/or Fear, Ending Manipulation, and other life-affirming topics.

Ilene is the author of *Emotions in Motion: Mastering Life's Built-in Navigation System*. She is a five-time Amazon bestselling author (three with The Wellness Universe's series on Self-Care) and has published more than 20 books, workbooks, and CDs. A frequent podcast and summit guest, Ilene appears on television and radio in the US and Australia.

As a child, Ilene lived in Germany and in Paris, France with her military family. She also summered on her grandparent's farm, where she learned at an early age to milk a cow, drive a John Deere tractor, skin a catfish, pick cotton (by hand) and can tomatoes. She is an ardent organic gardener.

Ilene's husband, neurosurgeon Dr. Robert Fink, died in 2016. A year later, she sold their home and bought a 24-foot RV, and has since roamed North America with her Maltipoo dog, Pi. A mother of six—two birth, one adopted, and three step—adult children—Ilene is a grandmother of five.

Ilene loves to talk. ilene@emotionalpro.com Let her know if you'd like her to swing by where you live to meet with you and your friends or family.

Connect with Ilene:

YouTube: https://www.youtube.com/@IleneDillon11524

CHAPTER 13

The Power of Oneness

LIVING FROM LOVE
AND TRANSFORMING RELATIONSHIPS

Laina Orlando, Awareness Coach

MY STORY

I don't know what I've gotten myself into, but I expect it to be magnificent!

What felt like my body was pulsing with aliveness. I was caught in the rhythm of a precise in-breath as all that surrounded me, the planets and the cosmos, collapsed into a stream of breath that filled me up and swallowed me. All that remained was pure stillness.

Immediately after the "ding-dong," Jan welcomed me into her home. Although we met once before, I didn't know what to expect from my first energy-healing session. Jan's home was charming, and I felt entirely at ease as I followed her to the healing room in the basement.

Now, five years into my healing journey, I've tried many healing modalities, such as psychic healers, inner child healing workshops, rebirthing processes, power animal journeys, shamanic journeys, lots of therapy, and many other experiences, each offering a unique piece of my healing puzzle. I was excited to experience my first energy-healing session sure I'd find another puzzle piece.

Jan pointed to her healing table. "Please remove your shoes and lie on your back." I felt excitement, curiosity, and deep trust.

I can't wait to start!

I settled onto the table as Jan gently placed one of her handmade quilts over my legs. "Close your eyes," she said once she sensed I was ready for the session. She began her process by standing by my head and asking permission to enter my energy field. Her gentle energy entering my field felt like a cool river flowing into the body of a warm lake. No longer sensing my body as solid, I relaxed and opened myself to receive. I entered a new realm of awareness I'd read about but now was starting to experience. I relaxed deeper on the table.

Here I go. But where to?

Within minutes, tears began to fill my eyes, and when the first teardrop rolled down my cheek, I knew my life would never be the same. As my hands touched the table, I felt my body levitating several inches from it. I sensed the outline of my body, but it was now fluid and light as a feather. I was both the observer and the participant.

This is fascinating!

I saw my body lifting as my head and shoulders became vertical while my feet remained inches from the table. I was now completely upright. As I traveled through a warm, silky mixture of never-ending darkness, I lost awareness of Jan's presence. Although my physical eyes were closed, I saw what I was sensing with precise details.

A point of light appeared in the distance. With my gaze fixed on the approaching light, I felt the same pure love as when my newborn children were placed in my waiting arms. This love was richer, familiar, and unfamiliar simultaneously.

As the presence came closer, its hands came forward to hold mine. I couldn't make out the face because the light emanating from this being was blinding. As the face emerged, my giddy inner eight-year-old recognized the approaching presence of Jesus because of my Catholic upbringing. As the being of light moved closer, I felt a loving parental energy surround me, and the essence of Jesus gave way to the presence of Mother/Father God. Although I was not religious, meeting God was lovely.

I was completely present in the experience as my five senses took in the sweet smell of family, the soothing sound of joy, the mesmerizing sight of love, the rich feel of eternity, and the delicious taste of peace. Then, a sixth sense kicked in, and I experienced melding with the light.

Suddenly, there was only Oneness. Yet I—my separate sense of self—was still present, knowing there was no I, only the Oneness of Is-ness. I began accessing deep, ageless knowing as everything about life and the universe came rushing into my awareness, and all made sense.

I was immediately drawn to a snake-like slithering ray of light moving up each of my legs.

WOW!

This light was alive and flowing toward my pelvis, coiling and filling my abdomen, lighting each chakra. The light paused at my heart chakra, reminding me: *It's time to remove all the obstacles you've built* and remember I Am Love and Light. The light was warm and thick like molasses as it moved from the throat chakra to the third eye and my crown chakra. I was then raptured into a swirl of energy from which flashes burst forth, instantaneously exploding into All That Is.

I observed everything manifesting as the light of my essence became every galaxy, each sun, moon, planet, and every star in the heavens. The visual shifted from the planets to the surface as mountains, valleys, oceans, lakes, and rivers, and I was each of them. Next, I was every person, plant, animal, blade of grass, and grain of sand. My vision was then drawn into every physical body, allowing me to know myself as the lungs, heart, ears, skin, veins, muscles, the smallest of cells, and the tiniest of atoms.

I Am, All That, I Am!

As I drank in the knowledge that I (and so are you) are the within and the without, the above and the below, the alpha and the omega, I experienced the power inherent in Oneness. At that moment, I felt humbled by my smallness while experiencing the peace and certainty of being the grandeur and infinitude of Creation.

What felt like "my" body was pulsing with aliveness. I was caught in the rhythm of a precise in-breath as all that surrounded me, the planets and the cosmos, collapsed into a stream of breath that filled me up and swallowed me. All that remained was pure stillness. Then, the exhale birthed all creation out of that stillness, and All That Is was placed in its perfect and precise place. Like clockwork, the rhythm continued.

Breathe in. Breathe out.

Every fiber of my eternal being was pulsing with the breath of life. I felt the power of eternal life that made death impossible. I felt the expansive and peaceful pulse of infinity.

Then, the unspoken dialogue began.

Dear God, since we are One, why are we taught that you are on a cloud somewhere far away and that we must jump through hoops to get close to you?

God replied: *My Love, you are playing a divine game of hide-and-seek. Oneness must appear separate so we can pretend to hide and seek each other. How else could we experience the joy of knowing each other?*

But God, why must this game include sadness and fear and often be painful?

My Love, it doesn't have to be, but because you and every one of your brothers and sisters are creators of your reality, you can each experience every frequency of the Love and the Light you are, including its absence. When you are playing hide and seek with the awareness that you are the Love and Light of All That Is, you experience joy, peace, and compassion for all beings. This is when you are vibing high and closest to your true nature. However, when you forget what you are by blocking the truth from your awareness with thoughts such as 'I am not lovable,' 'I am separate from others,' or 'I am not enough,' you automatically feel uncomfortable, tight, tense, small, dense, and alone. This contracted feeling was designed as the wake-up call in the game, but over many lifetimes, you have accepted the contraction as normal and made uptightness a thing. While you pretend to be separate in the game, most of you enter competitions for resources and play another game called haves and have-nots, which makes you believe in lack and limitation that gives rise to lying, stealing, cheating, and hoarding. Because you have been playing like this for so long, you have forgotten that it's just a game, and you act as if separation is real. But as you start experiencing Oneness, you realize life often felt like a nightmare while you were unaware of your power.

It all makes sense now, God!

You are so bright, My Love!

God, why did you wait until I was forty-two to start waking me up?

My Love, I was honoring your free will. You wanted to experience being deep in the dream by feeling abandoned by your parents, experiencing confusion about God and Creation inherent in religion, and having a few marriages, kids, and several careers as your reality. You also wanted to experience external authorities, so you idolized your parents, the government, bosses, and media personalities. You wanted to experience how it felt to trade your self-worth for the thrill of accumulating a net worth. And when you felt ready to leave the dream behind, the dismantling of the illusion of separation began with your mother's untimely death.

But that was five years ago, God. Why is it still so tricky to wake up?

My Love, fully waking is only tricky because you decide that what is solid and can be touched and seen is real, and what you can't see, or touch is not. Because everything is made of energy, you must go through a process of detaching from what you have come to believe is solid, and this is often painful because it is perceived as loss. The only reason you felt the meld with All That Is—Me—is because All That Is is My energy, and you Is That!

Ha, God, you are funny! Are more of us going to start waking up? After all, things are getting crazier on this planet.

Well, My Love, yes and no. Yes, because many of those experiencing the seeming separation have tired of being in hiding for many lifetimes. They are ready to be found and come out from behind the trees where they've been hiding. And no, because many still enjoy the game with low frequencies inherent when one chooses to hide their Light. The trick to awakening is to become courageous enough to feel the discomfort created by low-frequency thoughts and behaviors, whether they are called sadness, anger, guilt, or jealousy, and welcome the discomfort of the wake-up calls. Every time one of my children feels off and uses it as a sign to look inward, they become willing to see their beliefs about themselves and others that make them contract. By doing this, they can transform the shadowy lie into the Light of Truth that heals and frees them to live joyously and abundantly. As each of my children awakens, they no longer hide and become the torchbearers guiding their brothers and sisters out of the dense and dark hiding places. This is what being the Light of the world means.

Dear God, that doesn't seem like a fun game, so why would anyone choose to play it?

Well, My Love, as I said, you are the creators of your reality and enjoy adventures. Just as you did as a child, you played many games, some painful, like falling off the trampoline or getting burnt playing with fire. Each time you stop to review the games and their rules, you learn from your experiences and often revise the games if you desire a happier outcome. If you don't take time to go within and contemplate the game and its consequences, you don't learn from *it, so you repeat the process, hoping for different results. You call that insanity, and rightfully so.*

Oh, Dear God, how can we awaken sooner?

Well, My Love, this is why you are having this experience now: to remember the Truth of Creation by experiencing the awakening of your sleeping self, a process that may take another twenty years to complete. Once you remember that everyone is playing a game, you will lighten up for the game's duration. You will learn and advance as you teach what I guide you to remember. One day, you will learn from the very youngest to become like a little child, so those who are ready, and many will be in twenty years, will co-create a happy dream on planet Earth.

God, why twenty years?

My Love, because your planet is shifting into a New Age that requires those who want to up-level their game to live consistently from the higher frequency of Love. Because of your free will, everyone must choose Love over fear so the illusion of separation can give way to conscious co-creation. Over the next twenty years, those choosing awakening will activate their Light, illuminating the planet so all still hiding can see the consequences of their choices and choose again.

God, it sounds like the way to wake up is to become humble enough to realize what we thought was true might not be.

Yes, My Love. "The truth will set you free" when you humbly realize your thoughts are made up of the lies you believe and release yourself from them by choosing the Truth. You will quickly realize that you are playing a game of hide-and-seek with your mind and that you have the power to untether yourself from the shadowy lies that make you feel small, dense, and powerless. Then, you will begin to free your Light and live as the creators you are.

God, I am grateful for this wake-up call. I love you!

My Love, I love you more!

Tears flowed as I realized the oneness I experienced was our true reality. This truth has become a steady, loving pulse within me, reminding me daily that I am the creator of my reality.

I took my time wiggling my toes and feeling my body's weight on the table. The look on Jan's sweet face let me know she sensed I had a profound experience.

She doesn't know the half of it. Even if I told her, would she believe me?

Although I experienced a clear knowing of everything, my egoic mind created a fair amount of doubt and confusion for many years afterward. Because I trusted what I experienced, I put the tools I received into practice and began to transform. Although I'm still a work in progress, I'm constantly reminded that if I can do it, anyone can, including you!

Whether you're a young person, in midlife, or a wise elder, I shared my most profound experience with you. I hope my story activates within you a memory of who you really are: an adventurous old Soul like me.

THE PRACTICE

THE SHIFT AND LIFT PRACTICE

Awakening is not a one-and-done process but a practice that takes a lifetime to master. For this reason, give yourself some grace if you believe you have begun to awaken but still feel the egoic tendency to need to be right, judgmental, fearful, and guilty.

I received these four simple steps shortly before my meld with All That Is and can assure you that although I began practicing *Shifting and Lifting* from fear to love in 2007, I still use these steps daily. The secret to succeeding with this practice is to do the steps exactly as they are listed and not be tempted to allow your ego to alter them.

Select a comfortable, quiet space for this practice, and take a journal and pen or pencil. Remember that this is a powerful tool, and express gratitude for your willingness to do this deep inner work.

Here we go!

Everything starts with

1. **Awareness.** Contemplate your life and scan your thoughts. Notice and write down a person, place, or situation you wish was different. Acknowledge that you believe you'd feel better if that person, place, or situation changed. The ego always tricks us into believing others control our feelings, which is one way we give our power away.

2. Acceptance. Please answer with a simple Yes or No: Do you believe you can change *what is* or what *has already happened?* Radical honesty is key here.

3. It's time to Shift and Lift. You may feel awkward the first few times you do this step, especially if you do it exactly as instructed. Read what you wrote in step 1 and then notice the feelings and emotions that arise. Circle the five that best match your feelings under the Fear column. Be gentle with yourself if your feelings get intense. Next, under the Love column, circle the items directly opposite the Fear items you circled.

Love	Fear
Acceptance	Resistance
It is what it is – Neutral	judgment – Right or wrong
Expression	Suppression
Opportunity	Problem
Learn	Blame
Relaxed	Guarded – Anxious
Curious	Controlling
Clarity	Confusion
Defenseless	Defensive – Attacking
Forgive	Resent
Humor – Lightness	Grumpy – Heavy – Downer
Open	Closed Off
Confident	Insecure
Hopeful	Hopeless
Respond	React

Looking at each item you circled, scan your body and notice how you feel. Does your body feel at ease, peaceful, and light, or tight, tense, and dense?

My body feels: _____   My body feels: _____

Your body never lies because it is neutral. When we perceive life from love, we feel connection and oneness; when we perceive life from fear, we feel separation and disconnected.

4. I am powerful and decide how I experience life! Complete these statements and note what arises in your journal.

When I perceive "what is" with _____ (person, place, or situation) with love, I feel at ease, peaceful, and light, which causes me to experience connection.

When I perceive "what is" with _____ (person, place, or situation) with fear, I feel tight, tense, and dense, which causes me to experience separation.

The key to this practice is recognizing that when you perceive any person, place, or situation with fear, your ego is involved and will always cause separation because the game of life is being played unconsciously. However, when you perceive any person, place, or situation with love, your Soul/Spirit is involved and will always cause connection because the game of life is being played consciously.

It's time to forgive yourself for forgetting that only you can decide what to believe about anything. You have free will and ultimately control what you choose to believe. Your beliefs and perceptions always affect your feelings, creating your life experience.

This practice will help you become more self-aware, which can often feel uncomfortable. If you're committed to awakening, you'll welcome the discomfort as a sign you are *Shifting and Lifting* into a higher frequency, which is how transformation happens, and relationships, first with yourself, begin to heal and transform.

Now breathe. You did great!

Laina Orlando, a modern-day sage, offers a refreshing and engaging perspective on spirituality. Since 2007, she has been an Awareness Coach, Author, Founder of The Power of Awareness Program, and Director of The Awareness Academy. Laina is dedicated to helping others remember their God-given purpose: to experience eternal life, total liberty, and happiness.

Laina excels at distilling complex spiritual concepts into actionable insights that seamlessly integrate into daily life. Her spiritual awakening fuels her passion to share the limitless potential that awaits those who embark on the journey toward self-awareness. Recognized as a master teacher of A Course in Miracles, Laina humbly describes herself as an ordinary woman undergoing an extraordinary spiritual transformation. She firmly believes that if she can awaken, so can anyone else. Guided by her mantra, "Life is fun and easy!" Laina continues to inspire and empower countless truth seekers.

When Laina is not busy doing the work she loves, she is dedicated to sitting at the feet of her Gurus: three-year-old grandson Ryder and three-month-old granddaughter Ellie, whom she delivered during a heavy snowstorm that caused the midwife to miss Ellie's birth. Laina loves gardening, dancing, and getting into mischievous shenanigans with her girlfriends and favorite sister.

Laina is pleased to offer readers of Gifts of Wisdom a special gift:

The Soul's Journey is an introductory course to the expansive curriculum offered within The Awareness Academy. Please enjoy this 6-part Video Master Class completely FREE of charge as my gift to you.

https://awareness-academy.mykajabi.com/offers/2Kz9ib9C/checkout

Connect with Laina:

Website: https://lainaorlando.com/

Naba: https://naba.life/Laina

YouTube: https://www.youtube.com/user/LainaOrlando

Facebook: https://www.facebook.com/laina.orlando/

Instagram: https://www.instagram.com/lainaorlando/

TikTok: https://www.tiktok.com/@laina.orlando

CHAPTER 14

Beyond Limits

DISCOVERING YOUR WHY TO KNOW YOUR PURPOSE

Steve Halligan

MY STORY

The Tour Divide is the most iconic bike-packing endurance race on the planet, running since 2008. It's one of the longest and hardest. This is a no-frills set-up, no entry fees, no sponsors, and no prizes event. You sign up, get to the starting line in June every year, and follow the route to Mexico unsupported.

Simple, Right?

* * *

I swung my heavy mud-laden foot over my bike, clipped in, and pushed down on the pedals. A horrible sound of crunching metal and grit reverberated through my bike and pierced the silence of the damp, murky forest surrounding me. My upper body tensed as I looked back to the source of this unnatural sound. My rear derailleur was sucked into the spokes of the wheel, twisted and distorted, caked in mud.

What the fuck?

My head spun and my heart sank; despondent, I knew this was serious. I felt frozen; I took some deep breaths to calm my beating heart pounding in my chest.

* * *

The clock doesn't stop from the moment you roll out of Banff, Canada, and into the expansive wilderness of the Rocky Mountains. For safety reasons and so family and friends can follow along online, all riders carry a tracking device that updates exact locations at regular intervals to a specific website. This has become known as dotwatching.

The route continues on dirt roads and trails through Montana, Idaho, Wyoming, Colorado, and New Mexico. The route avoids busy highways and big cities; it's breathtakingly beautiful and diverse, showcasing a huge range of terrain and wildlife. This is a massive feat of endurance, so attritional that between 40 to 50 percent do not finish each year. Racers face everything from snowstorms to searing heat in the 4,200 kilometer journey. It takes its toll physically, mentally, and emotionally and isn't for the faint-hearted.

I got into competitive cycling relatively late, in my early 30s; I remember thinking that riding 100 kilometers was insane. Now, in these races, I ride between 250 and 350 kilometers daily—a huge perception shift.

In this race and others I've done I typically ride between eighteen to twenty hours a day, sleeping three to six hours each night. I often ride alone for the majority of the race.

I love pushing all my limits and facing my fears in different scenarios. I'm constantly learning and putting more trust in my physical and mental capabilities. I've experienced the highest of highs and the lowest of lows and always looked back with fond memories of each adventure.

This race became a huge catalyst for me to discover a true passion and unearth a deep purpose. It graciously filled a void in my life.

In the years leading up to it, I consumed blogs and videos and talked to previous racers. I was immersed completely in everything Tour Divide. I trained for months, I had big aspirations, I dreamed and visualized winning, and I was ready.

And here I was just 100 kilometers into the first day, looking down at my bike covered in peanut butter mud, chain dangling without purpose, and my rear derailleur hanging forlornly.

Only minutes earlier, I rode with vigour, still on the wave of adrenaline from the start.

Now what? Where exactly am I?

A long way from anywhere!

I've got to get my shit together and figure this out.

Many riders passed. Some shouted words of encouragement, others just rode by, head down into the cold rain. I removed the damaged derailleur and attempted to make my bike single-speed by shortening the chain. Various attempts were annoyingly unsuccessful. I was now wet, cold, angry, and frustrated.

Why me? Why did I have this bad luck on the first day?

My dark thoughts complimented the dark skies. I was in victim mode. Emotions ran high as I went from sadness to self-pity to fear. My ego ran the show.

I can't win now; it's over; I failed.

I took a moment; I breathed deeply to connect. I knew then I just had to move. I walked and walked up over endless hills and rolled down the descents as more and more racers passed me.

I reached Elkford, a tiny town a few kilometres off the route. Six long hours passed, and I was physically and emotionally wrecked. I checked into a motel, where a warm shower lifted my spirits.

The hours of pushing my bike had given me time to process and plan. My slower pace through the long evening hadn't gone unnoticed. My wife called me, and we chatted awhile before she suggested we take a few deep breaths together. She asked me, "Why are you there riding your bike?" Observing that I was still in my head, annoyed with my situation, she prompted me to remember, "It's exhilarating for you to be on your bike."

Before my tired body shut down for the night, I acknowledged this reminder and felt into my deeper why.

I was here for more than a high placing. I was here because I love riding my bike in wild places. I was here for the freedom that self-propelled travel allows and for the adventure my soul craves and consumes. I had to re-adjust my expectations and let go of self-inflicted pressure. I let go of my ego mind, surrendered to what is, and accepted it with a peaceful heart. I drifted into sleep with a more accepting mind.

I awoke early the next day feeling better and ready to do whatever it took to return to the race. I had to somehow get to Fernie, some 60-odd kilometres away, the nearest town with bike shops.

I stuck out my thumb; cars passed but did not stop.

After some time, my thoughts began to spiral. The petrol station cafe opened, and I needed caffeine, so I walked in. An elderly man began talking to me. "Hey there, Where are you going?"

"My bike broke down yesterday, and I need to get to Fernie to a bike shop to get it repaired"

"I can take you as I'm going there to visit my brother."

Forward momentum and a caffeine hit boosted my mood immediately. I was so happy. I threw my bike in the back of Alberts's truck, and we were off.

We chatted, and he shared many stories about his life. I thoroughly enjoyed my time and the opportunity to receive some healing elder wisdom from this engaging 84-year-old.

"I'll pick you up after your bike is fixed and bring you back to Elkford," Albert offered. *Amazing*—I gleefully accepted.

The rules of the race state that you have to rejoin the route where you left it, and that's what I did.

I was immensely grateful for the kindness of Albert and everything that transpired that day. I lost about twenty-four hours and well over a hundred riders passed me, but it was okay. My mindset shifted, and I saw the race through a new lens.

I rode out to rejoin the race route and felt tingles of excitement in my body. Hours passed over tough mountainous terrain before I rode back into Fernie, this time on two wheels and from a different direction.

Darkness descended and I rode out from the comforts of town and into the wilderness once more. With long distances between towns, these moments can be crucial. Aiming for a fast time will mean riding well into the night before stopping. Sometimes, however, getting a room in a town can be beneficial if the weather ahead looks nasty, as a cold, miserable night on a mountain can greatly affect your performance the next day.

I've been caught on high mountains in rain and snow and driving wind, where moving forward is the best option. Stopping can mean getting very cold with the possibility of hypothermia. Quality waterproof gear is crucial.

There are so many variables in these ultra-endurance races, and every decision has the potential to make or break your race. For this reason, being flexible and adaptable are key attributes to success. When I face some challenge or obstacle, I use the reassuring phrase: *This too shall pass.* It always does.

I was in grizzly bear country, so some discernment was required. I had some concerns about camping in bear habitats (new to me at the time), but I didn't let it paralyze me. I told myself that most wild animals prefer to avoid humans. I put up my tent and hung my food in a tree far from camp. Sleep came easy, only to be disturbed abruptly by my pre-set 4 a.m. alarm and not a bear, thankfully. I gathered all my gear, packed my bike and was off to climb two mountain passes before the U.S. border as the day's first light was gently illuminating the early morning skies.

The following days passed in a whirlwind of adventure and awe. After the disappointment of day one and the realignment of my soul mission, I was in a much better space. I never felt so strong on my bike, and I was supercharged with energy. I caught many other racers, brief chats ensued, and I pushed on down the spine of the great divide. It was enthralling. I rode my bike through stunning scenery, and I was propelled by joy and enthusiasm.

My stops for food and drinks were fast, mostly at service stations. I grabbed protein bars, nuts, bananas, and sandwiches if I was lucky. My vegetarian diet has some limitations for this kind of fast refuelling.

After the wet and cold weather of the first week, crossing into Colorado brought warmer temperatures. Now, over halfway into this monster ride, I'd moved up to sixth place. I was hugely empowered and motivated by what I had achieved thus far, but I also knew there was a long way to go.

Colorado has some amazing riding over big peaks, including Indiana Pass at 3,645 meters above sea level.

At some point most days, I was filled up with immense gratitude. It was such a privilege and honor to ride on these lands, experiencing so much every day out in the raw wild elements. I was humbled and moved to tears. I felt goosebumps and cool shivers on my skin under the warm Colorado sun—this is my kind of bliss.

Days passed by in a blur, days and nights interwoven, propelled by my strong desire and deep-rooted resilience. For the most part, I rode on a high. I handled the challenges in a flow state, garnered primarily from dropping into my deeper why. Everything is energy, and I tapped into an infinite source.

But there will be curveballs in races of this magnitude; circumstances can change in an instant. It's how you deal with them that decides your destiny.

In hindsight, I made the mistake of thinking of the finish too early—I mean, way too early. Entering the final state of New Mexico, my thoughts, at least some of them, went ahead to the end. This made me lose some focus, and I also began to feel fatigued. My pace slowed slightly but I was still going well—a prime example of the mind/body connection and its power.

New Mexico is spectacular, so diverse, rugged, and raw. I love it. It's notoriously hard and arguably the hardest section of the race. Long sections without resupply options, rough energy-sapping trails, extreme heat, and the potential for huge electrical storms all add to the spicy cocktail mix.

One of the many things I love about these types of races is I get to see all the sunsets and sunrises, and New Mexico puts on a magical show. The expansive arid deserts with distant mountain ranges capture the colors of evolving beauty magnificently.

After 17 days and 14 hours, I rolled into the finish. It was about 10 p.m., and I was alone at this remote border post. I slumped down to sit, listening to the deep silence, and looked up at the sky full of stars, still holding onto some orange hues from the recently departed sun.

I was exhausted, I was proud, I knew my life had changed, I had completed the biggest challenge I'd ever taken on. I had the biggest adventure of my life, and despite some very challenging moments, I overcame them and had a blast. I finished in fourth place.

I returned to this race again in 2019 and 2023 with more incredible adventures and many more tales to tell, but that's for another book.

THE PRACTICE

What defining events in your life have gifted you tools?

Have you recognized them and harnessed them to benefit you and others?

What I love about my ultra-endurance cycling journey these past ten years is that all I learned can and does translate to life. This race was one of my defining moments, and below, I've summarized five tools I learned and have since helped me countless times.

1. BREATHE DEEPLY

When the mud incident happened, and I realized I had a serious issue, I learned that taking some deep breaths calmed me down and lowered my racing heart rate. Utilizing slow, deep breaths to activate the parasympathetic nervous system helps reduce stress and promote relaxation, enabling a calm and focused state of mind.

There are various techniques but you can keep it simple. Inhale through your nose, filling your lungs so your belly moves out, and then exhale through your mouth, emptying your lungs. Repeat. Consciously doing this at any time is very beneficial for well-being as many people are unaware that they are shallow breathing most of the time.

Even though I was still in the middle of nowhere in the cold rain with a broken bike I was now in a much better state to make decisions to move on after some conscious breaths.

2. THE BIGGER 'WHY?'

Ask yourself the bigger "Why?" Reflecting on your deeper purpose and motivation and understanding the underlying reasons behind your actions can provide clarity, helping you stay committed and inspired during challenging times.

I had many hours to process my situation as I walked to the nearest town after unsuccessful attempts at fixing my bike. I looked at my predicament with a wider lens, which helped put things into perspective.

This sucks, and I'd prefer it if it was different, but here I'm in a new country, having an epic adventure, and it's only day one; it could be worse.

3. SURRENDER

Accept what is. Embrace the reality of your current situation. Accepting doesn't mean giving up; it means acknowledging the present moment without resistance, which can lead to calmness and the ability to respond effectively.

I realized resistance wasn't helping my mental state; my mood would deteriorate, and I just had to surrender to the moment. What you resist will persist.

Things didn't go as planned on day one. I had to completely change my expectations from ambitions to winning outright to simply finishing. My newly discovered deeper why changed everything, and I surrendered. I was there because I love riding my bike and the freedom it brings. I love the adventure, I love the challenge, and so much more.

There is nothing wrong with having big ambitions to win. If they come from a balanced place and a deeper perspective and not solely from ego, then they're okay.

4. ADAPTABILITY

Cultivate the ability to adjust and evolve in response to changing circumstances. Being adaptable allows you to handle unexpected challenges with grace and continue to progress without being derailed by obstacles.

These races throw up so many variables, such as weather, breakdowns, injury, etc., that I had to learn to be adaptable. If I was too fixated on outcomes I didn't achieve, it would eat away at me.

If I had dwelled on the fact that I may not win the race because I lost so much time, it would've been a very different experience and far less enjoyable. I've seen other racers struggle with this, so mastering it has been huge for me.

5. GRATITUDE

Being thankful. Practice gratitude by consistently recognizing and appreciating what you have and where you are. This mindset can enhance your well-being and keep you grounded and optimistic.

I've felt huge surges of gratitude that have brought me to tears whilst out there in the wilderness and solitude.

I've been practising gratitude daily for years now and understand its power. We often forget to be grateful, especially for the small things we tend to take for granted.

Take some quiet time to write a list of everything you are grateful for today, go deep and watch your list expand.

Can you see how these five tools can apply to many situations, and when practised and implemented, the outcome is sure to be enhanced?

I go deeper into all these practices and much more within my Holistic Endurance coaching program, and there are more insights and resources on my website www.selfpropelled13.com

Steve Halligan, currently living in New Zealand, continues to pursue his passion with Ultra Endurance cycling.

Growing up in rural Ireland, Steve developed a love of the great outdoors. Leaving Ireland at 21 years old broadened his horizons, and he got the travel bug, enjoying experiences that shaped him as a person.

A carpenter by trade, he worked in this profession until setting up a wellness retreat with his wife in 2015. An immensely fulfilling nine-year journey followed, delving deep into detox, yoga, meditation, massage, personal growth and so much more.

Now having moved on from the retreat, Steve continues to offer wellness services online and in person, including Holistic Endurance coaching, for people looking to achieve their dream goals, big or small; Steve will meet you where you're at.

His mission is to empower and mentor people to believe that they can achieve something that they thought was impossible.

Connect with Steve:

Website: https://selfpropelled13.com

Instagram: https://www.instagram.com/halligan.steve/

Subsstack: https://substack.com/@stevehalligan

Email: selfpropelled13@gmail.com

CHAPTER 15

It's Not Personal

HOW TO SHIFT SHAME INTO CONFIDENCE

Laura Di Franco, MPT, Publisher

"Shame is ridiculous."
~ Esther Hicks

MY STORY

Two powerful ideas helped me address the feeling of shame. One is that shame disappears when you call it out; you just have to be brave enough to get those words out loud. The other was the day I sat in the audience and listened to Esther's explanation of the three words in the quote above.

That day, sitting with two wonderful friends in the audience of that presentation, I was able to take radical responsibility for connecting to my bigger self, my essence, that part of me that is pure love. One of the huge gifts of wisdom that day was this: I decided not to take anything anyone says or does personally ever again.

Thank you, Universe! Freedom dropped in like a cool breeze. I felt like I had the secret treasure map to a life of joy.

Ask any psychologist—these aren't easy pursuits that I've declared for myself. But I love to ask these two powerful questions when life gets a bit hairy:

What if it were easy?

What else is possible?

As a lifelong learner, healer, and student of all things wild, crazy, and spiritual, I bask in new golden nuggets of awareness. "With awareness, you have a choice" has been my go-to quote most days, and it reminds me there's *never* a time (if I'm paying attention) that I don't have a choice in life. I learned the trick is to respond, not react, to events and moments. This requires a keen awareness of thoughts, words, and behaviors and the courage to change them when necessary.

Enter the worst triggers ever. You know, those kinds that hook you into a chaotic pit of Hell where you can't seem to stop perseverating on the nastiness?

I wonder if you, like me, share the one where when I think I've done something wrong (or worse, something that's made someone dislike me) and I cower into a messy puddle of low self-esteem and desperation and watch as the please-like-me behaviors start to happen without me feeling in control.

Oh, gawd, I feel sorry for that little girl right now. I love you, little warrior.

Recovering good girl, here. I know I'm not alone. Many of us spent our entire upbringing being taught what to say and how to behave to ensure we were being good. This, of course, was based on our parent's, teacher's, mentor's, and friends' versions of what was good behavior. It was confusing a lot of the time. Quiet, shy, self-conscious and afraid to speak was how I ended up most days in childhood.

Later in life, every time I made a goof, mistake or did something not quite perfect or acceptable, the feeling inside my body was so intensely visceral it felt like I'd die of shame. How did those triggers get so intense? The answer is complicated for most of us.

I won't go into the hundreds of amazing healing modalities available to help heal that ingrained (and many times subconscious) crap right now, but I'll tell you there are some magical mind-body-soul processes that greatly helped me reduce the not-normal reactions I experienced for decades. My 30-year career in holistic physical therapy gave me many gifts, but the most important was the knowledge of the breadth of alternative and holistic options I had when it came to feeling awesome and loving my life. Boy, did I dabble! I still do!

Nowadays, it's so nice to be able to observe a reaction happening inside me and then pause with a gigantic deep breath and choose something healthier. That's a ninja move of awareness! It starts with feeling your body.

There were 20 of us in the Kinesiology class at San Francisco State University. We gathered and huddled around the KinCom machine and listened as our professor shared about what it did. "You can measure the strength output of a muscle," he said as he got his volunteer student up onto the chair and positioned to test his quadriceps muscle. I looked down at the base of the KinCom, a machine we had in a clinic where I regularly volunteered, and noticed the lock mechanism was loose. So, helpful person that I am, I walked over and stepped my foot down on the pedal to lock it. Only, it was already locked, and I unknowingly unlocked it, causing the one-ton machine to slide a few inches on the floor.

"Stop! What are you doing!?" The instructor shouted, turning toward me and rushing over to lock it again.

You guys, it was like my parents had caught me with my boyfriend having sex for the first time—I instantly shriveled, my face flushed, and the wave of nausea was so intense I slowly backed myself toward the door of the small classroom and slipped out unnoticed. I turned my back to the cool white tile wall of the hallway and slowly slid down to the floor, putting my head in my hands until the nausea passed.

Have you ever noticed how shame feels in your body? Maybe not, because our first inclination is to shove it down, ignore it, or cover it up with something else as quickly as possible. I'm pretty sure I managed to press that feeling into some tiny crevice in my gut so tightly that it took decades to find its way to the surface and release.

If the professor responded differently, maybe with a chuckle and a, "Oh, no worries, I already locked it. Let's just lock it again," I would've been good to go. Instead, I carried that shame well into adulthood. But what the heck with that abnormal reaction?

What memories do you have that bring up a similar feeling? What are you making certain moments of your life mean? Do you still feel that feeling in your body even though there's no reason to?

My professor's reaction wasn't personal. It wasn't directed at me as a bad person. But when I heard the words and let that shock of the mistake I'd made, coupled with his intense shouting seep in, I was caught before I could practice the awareness I needed to create a different moment inside of me.

OMG, I'm so embarrassed.

They're all looking at me!

I won't be able to show my face in class again!

Maybe it's not too late for me to switch classes.

The truth is, everyone else was focused on the KinCom afterward, and nobody even noticed me leave or thought about it for another second.

Triggers happen in small, medium, and large ways throughout our lives. I often wonder what other kind of energy is lurking inside, waiting to be released from an old wound.

Another trigger I experienced was much harder to heal when it manifested after words were directed purposefully at me. This is another kind of challenge.

"This is your fault."

Four little words.

I got in the car after this very intense conversation and burst into tears.

Of course, this isn't your fault.

My inner wisdom tried to console me.

He's upset. He feels helpless. He has to blame you to feel better about it.

I listened, but it wasn't working. The knot in my throat choked me, and I called a friend to help me move through it.

"Maybe it *is* my fault," I sobbed.

"Remember, this isn't personal. He's reacting from his own filters. Everyone has lived a unique life from which they're reacting or responding to the moment. This isn't personal. Remember that."

She was a wise soul. I listened, and my heart softened a bit. My crying stopped, and I felt a surge of power inside. I took a bit of my power back in a few deep breaths.

"Nobody can make you feel any particular way," she continued. "Stay in your power. You know what you know. You know your truth, and that is enough. You don't need to explain it to anyone. You don't need to justify anything. And you don't need to apologize for anything. This wasn't your fault."

My inhale felt bigger than usual, like I'd forgotten to breathe for a few minutes and remembered again. I hung up and made the rest of the drive home with a bit less ruminating and more focused on power mantras that would help me shift my energy.

I love you, Laura.

You're a good person and a great mom.

You're one of the strongest people I know.

You're a beautiful, compassionate, caring badass.

Sometimes, your "call a friend" option is really important. When you're in the middle of a trigger, and the feeling catches you by surprise, you may find yourself falling into a pit of fear, despair, or darkness. The shame pulls you into yourself, and you watch as your body tries to get smaller—invisible. You're vulnerable, and in that state, it's hard to function normally. It's very hard to remember who you are. I probably shouldn't have gotten in the car so fast.

But calling a friend is a ninja move. It takes guts to reach out for help.

So is telling yourself, "I love you," when you feel like dying from shame. Self-forgiveness is probably one of the most powerful forms of self-love there is—also a ninja move.

After that happened I noticed how quickly I was able to recover. I was curious.

Maybe if we practice enough, we don't have to stay stuck or triggered for long at all.

I wondered this but, at the same time, knew it to be true. This can be instant. Your process can be quick as long as you're willing to pause, notice, breathe, feel, and then remember who you are.

I spent the rest of the drive practicing those steps. And by the time I was home, I felt back to normal, ready to take on my next moment, present, grounded, and centered in my power. The power of presence and the ability to stay in your body as the triggers happen is life-changing. It might even be the difference between a mediocre life and one filled with joy beyond your wildest dreams.

How about we practice together?

THE PRACTICE

SIMPLE BODY AWARENESS TO SHIFT SHAME

If I were to try to sum up the ultimate ninja move of awareness for you related to this topic of feeling triggered, I'd say it's a five-part process:

1. Notice

2. Breathe

3. Feel

4. Clear your mind

5. Remember who you are

Since this exercise only works in the middle of a trigger moment, I'll spell out the steps; then, it's up to you to practice pausing in the moment to catch yourself so you can put the steps into play.

The ninja levels of awareness happen when all five steps happen almost simultaneously, and the shift occurs in seconds. And that, my friends, will be palpable freedom for your life.

1. Notice

The very first step is noticing that you're triggered. "Hmm, will you look at that? I'm in a bit of a state, aren't I?" I really do try to keep it light when I'm talking to myself these days. Practice noticing. It will get easier and faster. "Hmm, that's interesting; I'm feeling so triggered right now." Be curious. Curiosity is an awareness superpower.

2. Breathe

In almost the same moment that you notice you're triggered, take a deep breath and keep taking deep breaths. If you begin to hold your breath, just move into the next deep, rib-expanding breath and carry on. Breathwork is an instant energy shifter and it will help you stay in your body while you practice the rest of the steps.

3. Feel

This may be the hard step. This isn't a technique where you hide, stuff, or ignore the feeling that your body is experiencing with the mental or emotional trigger. Triggers are mind-body. You won't heal it until you feel it. Notice, breathe, and feel. Where is the sensation in your body? What's happening? Breathe into that feeling and just be curious. Allow. Accept. Be gentle with yourself.

4. Clear your mind

Just like step 1 and 2 go together, so do 3 and 4. As soon as you begin to allow yourself to feel your body also clear your mind of anything you're making the feeling mean. Notice the thoughts like they are boats floating down a river, and you're on the bank watching them go by. Don't attach to them. Don't hop on to any boats! Keep breathing. Keep noticing. Keep feeling. And clear your mind. Notice one thought and then go back to noticing the sensations in your body and breathing through them and into them.

5. Remember who you are

This is the part when you've not only realized what's happening and created peace and calm within by breathing, feeling, and clearing your mind, but you add a little confident badassery. You are love, plain and simple. And love is the most powerful force in the Universe.

Remember who you are.

Remember your mission.

Beam love back into yourself, through your heart, and back out into the Universe. Allow other feelings and high-vibe energies like gratitude, joy, peace, or compassion to be the focus as you move from triggered to powerful and go about your purposeful day. You might try saying a power mantra out loud to amplify the moment. "I love you! You're a badass!"

My awareness practice has saved my life so many times. It's what keeps me healthy, joyful, hopeful, passionate, purposeful, and intentional about my life, even during the most challenging moments. I combine awareness with journaling to create a super-powered practice that heals whenever I need it.

For those of you wanting the next-level step, grab your notebook and pen, set a timer for five minutes, and write as fast as you can without censoring yourself. Fill in the blank. "I know who I am. I am _____. And what matters right now is _____."

And if you're feeling brave, email your writing to me at support@lauradifranco.com. Let me be a witness to the magnificent, wise, beautiful soul you are.

I write to Feng Shui my soul. I share to remember who I am and inspire you to be brave. The biggest gift you give yourself is to remember that all the wisdom you ever need is sitting inside you. Remember to breathe and feel—connect to that inner warrior.

Laura Di Franco, MPT, is CEO of Brave Healer Productions, an award-winning publisher for health, wellness, and business professionals. The publishing house includes Brave Kids Books and Brave Business Books and specializes in expert book collaborations. They offer programs that serve author-entrepreneurs well past their book launch.

Laura spent 30 years in holistic physical therapy (12 in private practice) before making the pivot to publishing. With 14 years of training in the martial arts, 13 of her own books, and a community of over 2000 authors (including over 80 Amazon bestsellers and counting), she knows how to help you share your brave words in a way that builds your dream business and life.

Her daily mission is to help holistic wellness professionals by paying forward everything she's learned in business and healing. She shares her authentic passion, wisdom, and expertise with refreshing transparency and straightforward badassery. Hold on to your seat because riding alongside her means you'll be pushed beyond your comfort zone and have way more fun with your purpose-driven fears.

When Laura chills out, you'll find her at a poetry event with friends, walking in the woods, driving her Mustang, bouncing to the beat at a rave, or on a beach in Mexico with something made of dark chocolate in her mouth. Joy is her compass and her business strategy.

Connect with Laura:

Website: https://BraveHealer.com

Free Facebook Group for Healers:
https://www.facebook.com/groups/YourHighVibeBusiness

LinkedIn: https://www.linkedin.com/in/laura-di-franco-mpt-1b037a5/

Good Morning Joy TV Episode:
https://youtu.be/vvYyMJGpP_U?si=Cbs5rTsbGRLsxfZS

YouTube:
https://www.youtube.com/channel/UCy5Ym97EetHuxpgJEHewwCQ

CHAPTER 16

Releasing the Habits of Anxiety

THE ART OF GRATITUDE TO TRANSFORM YOUR LIFE

Mary Jo Halligan CEO@Vibrant Love

MY STORY

I want to be asleep and not have to do this human life thing today.

I awake reluctantly after a rough night of tossing and turning before sleep finally took hold. The energy rushes to my head as the pressing thoughts squeeze my brain. My muscles become agitated with dull aches and tension.

The thoughts demand more of my attention as my sensitive nervous system tilts into sympathetic overdrive, ringing the resounding alarm bells of *doomsday alert, danger, danger*. In my attempt to distance myself from all the noisy chatter and uncomfortable sensations, I turn over onto my right side, pulling the cozy, warm bedcovers over my shoulders: *Maybe it's just a bad dream.*

I resist getting up as I cling desperately to the warmth of my cocoon.

Fuck I hate this feeling of desperation. What the fuck was I thinking anyways? Why do I seem to mess things up with my big ideas? Who do I think I am to believe I can change my life and live my dreams in peace, joy, and harmony?

Whose bright idea was this to throw myself into this deep hole and trust I'd find a way out? Oh yeah, it was mine!

I feel sickly with a heaviness in my abdomen area. I don't want to move an inch, and I can't stay still as my thoughts rage, spinning me out of any restfulness.

How nice it would be to wake up again and discover it was all a nightmare I imagined. I welcome that kind of relief right now.

It seems so ironic to find my body semi-frozen like a deer caught in the headlights; the fear feels crippling.

My intention and desire was to muster the courage and faith to stretch myself into new, empowering ways of thinking and behaving. I wanted to explore new possibilities that excited my heart by living more authentically and moving in the direction that felt most liberating. I wanted to believe I could become a more empowered version of myself who wasn't constantly fighting off and trying to manage self-doubt and self-worth issues.

Even with all the years of travelling, yoga, meditation, massage, and healing modalities, here I was, juggling with the same old crappy thinking patterns and nervous energies I dealt with in my childhood.

I still felt like that overwhelmed little girl who grew up on a little farm on the west coast of Ireland, spending three of those formative years in two different children's homes. Yet here I was, still trying to hold it all together, feeling burdened and under-resourced. The difference was I was thirty-one years old and living my life on the other side of the globe in New Zealand.

Over the years, I did my best to release the habits of anxiety by discovering new ways to live my life. I learnt to take risks when I was unhappy by doing things out of my comfort zone. I choose to follow my heart instead of heeding the fearful thoughts of my monkey mind. I often made decisions that made no sense to my logical mind and leaned into trusting my inner senses to guide me.

I knew obsessive worry was such a shitty tool for life, but that was what I picked up in my childhood. Worrying and my stomach churning into knots was still a default habit I was working to shake out of my subconscious patterns. I feared deep down I had messed things up so badly and done something unforgivably wrong.

Accompanying the worries were the crushing thoughts about my future. I cared far too much about other people's judgments and opinions. I chanted loudly to counteract this, "What other people think about me is none of my business!"

As I lay in my bed dealing with the discomforts in my mind and body, I focused on my breath to try to relax and slow the thoughts down: Maybe I can create some space between the bumper-to-bumper thoughts to get a moment's peace.

As I followed the inhale of my breath and exhaled, old memories from my childhood connected to the body sensation I experienced rose like a phoenix into my mind's eye. I held the vision of my 11-year-old self and my first and only hospital visit.

After what seemed like a long night of discomfort suffering from abdominal pains and cramps, my father drove the 20-minute journey to take me to see the local doctor, who said, "Get her to the hospital right away!" At the hospital, they held my little body down to extract blood samples from my spinal area as a nurse whispered in my ear, "Don't be a crybaby." They never did figure out what was up with me, even with all the blood tests.

As a young child, I had an inner sense I'd need to discover how to heal myself in this life. By age nine or ten, I knew I didn't want to end up like my mother, whom I witnessed living what seemed to be a very unsafe and unhappy existence travelling to and fro to stay at what was called "the mental hospital" back then.

By age 14 or 15, I knew I did not prefer to end up like my father either. He seemed consumed with regret and bitterness for not having the courage to follow his dreams and create a better life for himself when he was younger and had the chance.

After my 11-year-old childhood memory subsided, another one surfaced to take its place. This time, I was aware of myself as a child at primary school on another day when I experienced intense cramping pains in my abdomen. With the level of discomfort I experienced, it took every bit of my focus and energy to hold it all together and pretend I was okay. I dared not let on that something was up with me. It wasn't that the teacher was mean, even though he could be. It was that I perceived I had no one I could confide in without causing a fuss, and I avoided any kind of spotlight focus on me.

Thankfully, I discovered a way to help myself to reduce the pain. When the lunchtime bell rang to alert the students to return to class, instead of heading back in with everyone else, I stayed in the girl's bathroom. It was located in the schoolyard in a separate building from the classrooms. With no one around and the schoolyard quiet, I laid my body down on my back. As I did this, the sensation of the cool concrete floor took over my attention. I brought all my focus onto my breathing. As I did this, I noticed the gripping cramping pains decreased, and I could return to class with relative ease to get through the rest of my day.

A sudden thud echoed, and instantly, my attention was firmly back in my bedroom. The childhood memories dropped away, dissolving back into wherever they came from. I looked in the direction of where the thud came from and noticed a bird crashed precariously into the window. This timely distraction helped me become present enough in my body to make the assertive decision to get out of bed and have a shower. No more thinking, I proclaimed; let's get moving!

As I moved my body in the direction of the ensuite bathroom, a new wave of panicked thinking rattled my nervous system with the reality check that reminded me: You're in *$65,000 worth of debt*. What was worse was the bitter shame I felt as I had risked borrowing that money and then proceeded to give it away to a network marketing company. I joined the company because it held the promise of freedom if I followed their lead and achieved the entrepreneurial and financial success stories they promised.

Before I arrived in New Zealand a year and a half earlier in 2008, I travelled around Costa Rica in Central America with my partner. One day it became shockingly clear that my heart was done travelling. The message I received went something like this: It's time to stop being a fly on the wall and do something with all you've learnt with all of your life experiences.

Two months later, I arrived in New Zealand on a one-year working holiday visa. Even before the plane started its descent into Auckland airport, and knowing this was our first time visiting this country, I turned to my partner Steve and declared, "Welcome home." In Auckland City, we bought a camper van. Over the following months, we drove southward and eventually entered the little alpine village of Hanmer Springs.

It was wintertime, and we needed work and a roof over our heads. I was delighted to be offered work as a massage therapist at the local Thermal Pools and Spa within an hour of our arrival. By that evening, we moved into a house where we found a spacious room to rent.

Within a few months of working at the local day spa, I started to feel my passion for working as a massage therapist decline. I needed to leave the job before all the passion got squeezed out of me. However, the only way I knew how to make money was to be an employee. Business ownership was never role-modelled to me growing up nor did I know anyone at that time who owned a business either. Yet the feeling nagged my heart that I had the potential to start my own massage business and create it in a way that sang to my heart and soul.

That led me to sign up with the network marketing company to learn how to think and act more like a businessperson with an entrepreneurial spirit and a millionaire mindset. I took the initial leap of faith and invested $3000 NZ to receive the first personal development product the company offered. I attended the weekly training calls, which were helpful over those first few months. If only I had left it there and trusted that was all I needed from that company to set sail on my entrepreneurial visionary path.

The real issue was my lack of trust in my capabilities married with self-worth and self value issues. My suffering came from this inner conflict of push and pull, yes and no, heart and head in a tug-of-war instead of agreement.

A big a-ha moment of profound clarity I received from getting myself into such a debt hole was: passion doesn't follow money; money follows passion. I learnt the hard way that I had to stay true to the deeper visions and guidance of my heart no matter what. Money didn't drive nor inspire my heart and soul; passion did, and I had a passion for caring for people's well-being and empowering their spirits.

As I stood in my warm shower feeling the nurturing caress of the water cascade over my shoulders and down my back, a flicker of hope whispered: *I will get through this.* Just then, I turned to my right and saw the sticker on the shower tiles that shone out to me as I read the words, "What AM I grateful for today?"

In that moment, gratitude wasn't what I experienced. I repeated the question out loud to myself a second time. "What AM I grateful for today?"

Again, I wasn't feeling much to be grateful for and everything to be uneasy about. When I asked the third time, I felt a softening in my body and breath. I took a sigh and released my breath. I spoke out loudly: "I AM grateful I remembered to take a breath." As the warm water flowed over my body, I spoke out loudly again, "What AM I truly grateful for today?"

This time I responded, "I am grateful for my shower, I am grateful for the warm water in my shower, I am grateful for the roof over my head. I am grateful for my cozy bed, I am grateful for my lovely bedroom and my bathroom, I am grateful I have food in my kitchen and get to make different food choices about what I have for my breakfast."

As I spoke these words out loud, the tightness in my body softened, I felt more spaciousness and a sense of relief, and I breathed easier. The more genuinely grateful I became for what I already had, the more relaxed and at ease I felt. The weight of the overwhelming mental and emotional dark clouds promising treacherous storms lifted.

My energy shifted out of the grip of the rushing, colliding fears. I was ready to take it to the next level. I took another conscious breath and opened my Louise Hay Power Thoughts Affirmation book intuitively to the page, "I am safe where I am; I create my own security." On the second page, it read, "I trust myself, and I trust life to support and protect me."

I closed my eyes and allowed myself to feel the impact of each affirmative word and sentence as I repeated them. As I did this, tears shed from my eyes and streamed down my cheeks, releasing the old cellular memories. Each time I repeated the affirmation, I welcomed the empowering new thoughts and energy frequency as I inhaled deeply my breath. With each exhale, I released more outdated limiting thoughts, beliefs, and associated energy frequencies.

Once I felt ready to move on, I invited myself to imagine what it might feel like to experience the feelings I truly desired to feel. As I swayed my body from side to side, holding the power thoughts affirmation book close to my heart, I imagined the feelings of my life filled with wonderful opportunities, divine security, joyful connections, and supportive resonances that delighted my heart and soul.

I dared myself to imagine what it might feel like to run my thriving massage business filled with a steady flow of grateful clients overjoyed with the services they received. I imagined my clients feeling more than happy to make the financial payment exchange knowing that their massage experience had exceeded their expectations. I imagined what it would be like to share open-hearted hugs and warm smiles with them before they departed.

As I kept playing with these kinds of imaginations and feeling frequencies, I felt more secure that all was well in my world, even if my logical mind had no idea how. I accepted that "the how is none of my business."

Nothing beats experience to help you discover what works for you or not. I realised how powerful the practice of gratitude truly was in transforming my life. It has become an integral part of my daily rituals to support and enhance myself with abundant thinking energies.

Whatever you focus on grows, so the more you focus on things to be grateful for, the more your abundant thoughts and feelings grow within you. Along with the practice of gratitude, my daily wellness toolkit included choosing one or more of the following: affirmations, yoga, meditations, salt baths, dancing, walks in nature, oracle cards, journaling, authentic conversations, healthy yummy foods, intuitive life coaching, and taking inspired actions from my heart.

As the following weeks and months passed, I continued to set up my massage business. Over the next few years, my business grew with rave reviews from my clients. My Mountain View Massage business became the No.1 rated day spa on Trip Advisor in Hanmer Springs village. A few years later, the opportunity opened up for myself and my partner Steve to launch our joint dream of running a wellness retreat and day spa together in 2015 which we did for nine years.

THE PRACTICE

The art of gratitude to transform your life is really about meeting yourself exactly where you are with this profound and simple tool. It's not about being a nice and good person pretending to be grateful when you're not.

Practising gratitude artfully is a bit like being a caring parent dealing with a scared little child. The art of gratitude is gently taking the hand of that child and guiding them over to where all the good stuff is happening. Before long, the child starts to forget what they were upset about. The fears and tears get replaced with more joy, laughter, and creative imagination.

Step 1. Ask yourself: "What Am I truly grateful for today?"

Step 2. Ask yourself the same question again until you feel your awareness shift onto something you are genuinely grateful for in your life.

Step 3. Keep speaking out loudly about what you're grateful for until you feel a tangible shift in your energies and thought processes. You'll notice your body is more relaxed and spacious.

Step 4. Choose another helpful practice from your wellness toolkit, or visit my website www.maryjohalligan.com for great tools.

Step 5. Know and accept that you are worthy! You can transform your life to follow your heart's desires and live your highest joy.

Mary Jo Halligan grew up in Co, Mayo, on the west coast of Ireland. In 2008, she arrived with her partner Steve in New Zealand. In 2010, she developed her massage business in Hanmer Springs. In 2013 and 2014, she trained in Quantum Healing Hypnosis Technique. In 2015, along with her husband Steve, she launched her yoga and detox wellness retreat vision called Vibrant Living Retreat & Day Spa, which was sold nine years later in December 2023. In 2017, Mary Jo launched Vibrant Wellness Academy to train and certify her students in holistic, intuitive massage. In 2024, life is in transition, developing online resources and courses.

Connect with Mary Jo:

Website: https://www.maryjohalligan.com/

https://maryjohalligan.substack.com/

CHAPTER 17

Starting Again

A SPIRITUAL PRACTICE FOR MOVING FROM COLLAPSE TO HOPE

Frank Byrum

MY STORY

On the whisper of a spring breeze, the smell of mint was the aroma—clean, refreshing, and clearing.

Deep breath, inhale—slowly, one, two. Hold, one, two. Exhale, one, two. Inhale. . .

Sweet basil, memories sleepily drifting to pesto with garlic, no, Caprese salad.

Yum.

Breathe in—slowly, no, slower, slower. My shoulders fall, and the relaxation ripples down my spine.

The floral, woodsy, herbal smell of lavender.

Focus drifting, a tiny buzz, then two, and more—a chorus, no, a symphony, just over the fence.

There is an ancient tradition known by many names.

Joseph Campbell said it was the hero's journey to follow your bliss.

Richard Rohr ascertained it in his book's title *Falling Upwards*.

From Homer's Iliad and Odyssey to modern times, this narrative is likely as old as human history, retold for generations around a nightly flame.

Breathe out, slower, slower—one, two, three, four.

A sip—*spring grass and floral and mildly astringent.*

2024 Indian Darjeeling, first flush, picked early spring after the winter and before the monsoons.

The early birds are chirping, and the sun has yet to cast the long shadows of morning.

Breathe in—no, slower, slower, no, slower.

Somewhere between the sleepy awake from the dream world and the real day—the thinning of the veil—each morning starts with ritual.

Often, events of years or days past stream past my thoughts like an odd, twisted, and seemingly unrelated tapestry. My belief—the spilling over of the unconscious mind into the transition to waking.

How the hell does a 16-year-old write a computer language? A memory from my junior year of university meeting a new student, John, days before class. He's clicking away in a computer lab, alone.

I feel so dumb.

Many traditions recount the same truths found in the Vedas, the Tao Te Ching, the Gateless Gate, the Gnostics, and the Bible with the Apocrypha.

The same old story—rinse and repeat—Adam, Enoch, Job, Abraham, Isaac, Moses, David, Jesus, Peter, Paul.

The narrative structure is essentially the basic template of life's journey.

How it works and how it breaks. The mountain highs and the deepest valley.

The lesson, the heartbreak, the reality.

Isaac's son Jacob is an exceptional example as well as Jesus' parable of the Prodigal Son.

Breathe out - slower still.

Congratulations for shipping your first software. I can see my embarrassment of recognition as I downplayed the attention. Although, I'm ashamed to admit there was a crack of a hidden smile upon my lips.

Life's journey unfolds in three simple vignettes, often repeated seemingly in loops as each essential lesson is learned, forgotten, and relearned with a nuance.

PHASE 1—BUILDING IDENTITY AND EGO

Life essentially starts the same for everyone: birth, domestication by parents, family, and extended family, socialization by close family, friends, and society, and sometimes, religion or other cultural artifacts.

I was raised an obedient, disciplined, studious, hardworking, conservative Southern Baptist.

Rules.

Do's.

Don'ts.

Sin.

Hell.

Where is the love and grace?

Then comes early grade school and the early cruelty of childhood teasing, which seems to continue in different forms throughout life.

I was different—soft, reflective, and intuitive. Punished into the desired mold. Secretly, my soul seemed to have little in common with my parent's microcosm.

Middle school was worse. My sense is that those early teasers often become bullies and worse as life unfolds into adulthood.

"I'll pick Bobby"

Three left; pick me. Please, pick me.

"I'll pick Frank."

Breathe out.

I visualize my uncomfortable smile and the emotional relief of not being picked last.

Breathe in.

For the earlier years of psychological development and through the first 20, maybe mid-30s, the essential identity is formed and solidified:

Who are your family, your friends, your school—especially in high school and university?

What your religion and political beliefs are.

For Jacob, Isaac's son, his identity is associated with "The God of my Father Abraham and the God of my Father Isaac."

Do you see what's missing?

What about Jacob's God? It was his father's God, not his God.

And that often sums up my early development—it was my parents' everything and I had to unlearn and earn my everything.

In the parable of the Prodigal Son, seemingly unhappy with his life, he said to his father—"Give me my inheritance." His identity—a rich kid looking for adventure.

Which, in a way, happened to Jacob when he ran away from his brother Esau.

A distant memory—"Where are your pictures?"

I flipped over to the endless rows of faces. Embarrassed—I was the guy who was missing throughout the high-school annuals. As the fourth child, there were few pictures of me before I became an adult.

I was creative, curious, and a deep observer. I was different, very different, and asked difficult questions—nominally pointing out the hypocrisy and rule-ignoring of all those "godly friends" and my parents.

"Science, you are good in science, and that should be your focus," said Mom.

Breathe out—a long, slow sigh.

The memories flood into my meditation, and I press into the agonizing flow.

Depression-era parents have no use for creatives and even less for intuitives.

For a moment, realizing my breathing, I paused, attempting to hold back the torture.

Breath in - slower - longest yet.

Words are spells. Yes, word-spells.

In youth we begin to receive such spells and it's a lifelong endeavor to identify these limiting beliefs and reverse each.

I've believed many word-spells versus trusting my heart and intuition. Remember, *domestication!*

"Mr. Byrum, it appears you have bled on this essay." Mr. Holbrook said in tenth-grade English.

I told myself: *I'm never going to be a writer.*

Sure, I could write technical, but never anything else.

This was a nearly 40-year word-spell I broke during COVID when I took my first adult writing class.

The goal of those first 30-ish years is identity and ego, with all the self-imposed limitations and word-spells thrown as an extra burden.

Breathe out.

Silence, finally!

Breathe in.

Who am I? No. Who am I, really?

So many masks, so many people—all rolled into a single chameleon. I learned to be who was demanded—a shapeshifter different at home, family, work, church, and with each "friend."

PHASE II—THE STRUGGLE

Many traditions claim this is a lesson or a chain of related lessons. Or the Universe's mirror. Others claim it's karma or causality.

I know many claim it's God's divine judgment and thus deserved. Cosmically, if they happened to be pious believers, it's the Devil's oppression.

In all cases, the struggle is a major life event, often traumatic, or many smaller events leading to a crescendo.

These deeply challenge my identity and everything I believe to be true, right, or just.

The vase of life is shattered, the shards so broken—there is nothing to hold back the porcelain tears.

Reality sets in. Oddly, it' was much later in life that I began to understand that arguing with reality is a losing battle 100 percent of the time.

Death of a father, my wife's miscarriage, her affair, separation, divorce, loss of friends, ostracized from a religious community, selling the house, a job loss, then rejections, then finding a new job, financial debt, buying a new house, a mother with dementia.

Breathe out.

Jacob ran away. So did the Prodigal Son.

I wanted to run away, too. I was in DC, 200 miles from home, driving west and kept driving for nearly an hour.

The plan. *Stop by the bank, get some money. Leave a voice mail and abandon the house and all assets else to my first wife. Another state and start over.*

I was overwhelmed, depressed, and emotionally exhausted.

Then it hit me: maybe there was something I was missing—the mental recording that played both night and day.

I was 46. That list above? That was four years of my life!

For most everyone, the valley seems to come from late-30s to late-40s.

Breathe in and breathe out. Too long. It took a while before I was breathing regularly again, and I could regain composure to meditate.

Drifting, a recollection—on my knees, begging.

Let her return. Please, make her see.

God, are you there?

This wasn't the deal. This wasn't the promise. It should be different. I followed the rules, was an overall good guy, a solid worker, went to church. I was a Sunday school teacher, a deacon, a servant, tithe giver.

Do unto others. Right?

I checked every box. My belief was simple: if I lived the rules, I'd receive the blessings.

Breathe in.

Doesn't God, the Universe, reward the good and punish evil?

PHASE III—THE DECISION

Who am I?

Am I all the misfortune, all the achievements?

Am I what she says?

Am I the lies they believe?

Both?

Am I any of this?

It's all your fault - you are an angry and verbally abusive man.

This word-spell bounced around my meditations for months, and I relived the filmstrip endlessly in my dreams. At 3 a.m., these were the first words remembered on my way to the bathroom and before attempting to return to sleep again.

This word-spell, along with the related traumas leading up to separation and divorce, resulted in years of insomnia.

Breathe out.

The words of a past lover cut deep

That spell took years of therapy to undo—trying to fix what wasn't broken.

On my darkest day—the day I thought might be my last.

My mental conflict, each inner voice was shouting, a repeating voice, and each word-spell was strengthened by the retelling and the daily cycle.

I didn't need the humans anymore. The word-spells were so ingrained that I was perfectly capable of torturing myself with no one in my life.

Live or leave?

Love or hate?

Yet.

Yet, there was a much deeper voice speaking to me. A me I once knew. I remember, vaguely, like the smell of mint.

The professional accolades, the awards, the interviews.

All the times I taught Sunday school and Bible studies.

What did it all mean?

All the shit I have achieved. My resume and stories. Meaningless.

Focus. Breathe in - slow, fill the belly.

There are many names for a higher essence—God, Lord, Universe, Tao, Source, Spirit. For me, there is no word that seems to capture the truth. Each name tries to box the un-boxable, bind the un-bindable, and define the indefinable.

For the last phase, please use the divine name that works for you.

For me, Spirit works.

Jacob wrestled the angel. The Prodigal's epiphany occurred while feeding pigs.

For me—I was crying, walking through an empty house.

I cared for nothing.

I wanted nothing.

It was all so meaningless.

. . .Seek, and you will find. . .

This simple idea, among many related ones, filled my consciousness, and that day, I made an odd decision.

My blessed days, my most blessed days, are ahead of me.

Breathe out.

Imagine, after those four horrible years, dreaming up such an idea.

Thank you, Spirit!

Whether it's a sequence of smaller losses or a life collapse, we each have a choice. The choice is simple: double down on identity and ego or open your heart and seek an essence greater than all the woes of life's.

Psalm 119:105 states, "Thy word is a lamp unto my feet, and a light unto my path." (KJV)

I believe this to be an essential prayer. Ask for the next step, a word.

Surprisingly, a next step has always appeared—albeit it's often "wait."

Faith is the step beyond the light of the lamp.

The journey transformed—from my identity and ego focused solely on the destination (I call this destination thinking) into a step-by-step faith journey.

Reading the omens and signs along the way.

A honeybee buzzes by.

Breathe in lavender. There is nothing equal to lavender on the bush.

Memories rush forward—mistakes one after another, those who have wronged me— everyone I blamed, each a past tormentor.

These reflections, these hungry ghosts, appear much less these days, although a visit signals a word-spell not fully broken and replaced or a new word-spell attempting to take root.

Life isn't fair.

The good guy doesn't always win and get the girl.

The cowboy doesn't always ride into the sunset.

Jacob returned home and was accepted by his brother, Esau.

The Prodigal was welcomed by his father with a ring, a robe, and a feast—and scorned by his brother. Maybe the brother who refused to celebrate his return was the true Prodigal Son?

If you wait long enough, you'll see the heart of a person, and it may take half a lifetime to see your own heart.

Breathe out. One, two, three, four. Breathe in.

So where are you these days?

Have you noticed that those elders, later in life—bitter, angry, and out of sorts with every detail of life? My speculation is they continued to double down on identity and ego and refused the signs, omens, and ultimately, the Spirit.

If the chance for early-life correction is ignored due to emotional, identity, or ego resistance, the chips keep stacking up, leading to greater carnage and regret later in life.

Could they be living Hell on Earth?

It was later when Jacob seemed to have his own God; it wasn't the God of his fathers, but his God.

He earned Spirit, or rather, he proved the existence of Spirit through trials and tribulations.

And I believe this is the lesson. This is the template of life. This is the journey of life, repeated throughout.

Consider the Prodigal's brother—was he doubling down on his identity and ego?

I'm humbled to report those blessings did emerge, and for over a decade, I've enjoyed blessings with a loving partner, and all that was taken away was returned in right relationship to Spirit.

I'm still seeking. I refer to myself as a mystic—with a broad view of spirituality and a growing compassion.

To close this story, let me ask a few questions:

What phase are you in your journey?

Identity and ego?

The valley?

Doubling down?

Looking for an answer?

I hope this chapter reminds you that you are human, living a human experience.

Your ups and downs are real and normal. While the details differ, the journey is essentially the same.

Your emotions are information—important signals attempting to get your attention to slow down to…

Smell that lavender. I do love lavender.

Breathe out.

Buzz, buzz, buzz.

The bees know, too.

THE PRACTICE

Allocate a least two hours without any following planned activities. I recommend at least a 30-minute post-exercise buffer, specifically so you can keep going if necessary. When initially starting, it's important not to be emotionally rushed by your next appointment.

Find the quietest place possible, in nature or a park or a quiet room. Use noise-canceling headsets as a last resort.

This initial work will take several sessions; try not to feel rushed. Rushing to another task is an easy form of avoidance.

In my focus, I brew a small pot of tea, bring a pen and writing pad, and sit outside, away from distractions.

Remember, this is a paper exercise. Turn off or store your computer and cell phone. No cheating, this will distract from your full attention to the initial recovery diagnosis.

Double check, no cellphone, right? No dings or alarms, right?

Brain chatter is normal. Don't fret, don't resist, embrace the chatter: today's to-do list, meetings, memories, anger, anything. Give yourself permission to attend to these later and write each on the pad as they appear.

Start with a memory and let the chatter vomit onto the page with no editing. Write as fast as possible and let it all out.

When your brain silences, get a red pen and try to summarize in a few words for each section of blather. Perfection and precision don't count; just try to capture the basic idea in a word or two.

Take a deep breath, filling the lungs from the bottom to the top. Let out a slow, long sigh through your mouth. Repeat this process two additional times.

Place your hands on your heart. Take another slow, deep breath, and with a sigh, let it out a few seconds longer than your inhale.

Ask the following questions:

• What do I need to know? Give yourself time to hear the response.

• What is my next step? Give yourself time to hear the response.

Don't be overly concerned if the chatter overwhelms the direction. This process takes time and practice. Realize that "wait" might be an answer.

Give yourself several sessions, maybe a few weeks of a similar exercise. Also, look for signs and omens, specifically anything that seems to align with your answers.

If you are strong-willed, don't be surprised if you hear (from yourself) what you want to hear. Sometimes, the will is so strong that I've taken an action and failed before I could hear what was really being taught.

It may seem gratuitous to suggest that you take care of yourself. A wise friend taught me that "the leaning fence post falls first."

Don't neglect your daily practice. This is the first step; please visit my website for ideas and resources and send me a note on how it's going.

Frank Byrum is an inventor and scientist, technologist, and bestselling author who has spent the last four decades on a spiritual journey, the last few of which have been focused on deep self-healing. His dad led his early spiritual training in the Southern Baptist tradition, and following in his footsteps, for several decades he continued the family tradition as a Bible teacher.

To continue his religious education, he began a Master of Theology in Apologetics, and it was during this time that he began to consider the teachings deeply and realized few taught or even mimicked Jesus' love, kindness, and healing. Ultimately, not completing the degree and with this soul-belief—*what was once known and practiced has been lost.*

This questioning, this crisis of faith, led to decades of searching various wisdom traditions and teachers, and with a simple faith believing the promise of Mathew 7:7— *"Ask, and it shall be given you; seek, and ye shall find; knock, and it shall be opened unto you"* (KJV).

For years, he has shared his understanding with friends, family, students, and associates as he continued to research and practice. He earnestly believes everyone can benefit from the foundation of practical daily practice, and it's the best way to *"be in the world, but not of the world."* Today, his daily practice includes tea, breath work, prayer and meditation, martial arts katas, Qi-Gong energy work, and wisdom studies. He resides in southern Virginia, where he practices, teaches, and writes.

Download a PDF of the exercise and a guided audio: https://themindfulpathway.com

Connect with Frank or send him a note.

Website: themindfulpathway.com

Email: frank@themindfulpathway.com

Twitter: https://twitter.com/MindfulPathway or @MindfulPathway

Instagram: https://www.instagram.com/tfbyrum

CHAPTER 18

Master Your Energy Matrix

A GUIDE TO PERSONAL AND SPIRITUAL FULFILLMENT

Virginia Rounds Griffiths, Dip CHt, Dip LFP, Ct NLP

MY STORY

My thoughts flew to my mother, who was miles away and previously had lost two precious daughters at birth. My little mind was very aware of the devastation my drowning would cause her. Now, seven decades later, every one of those slow-motion frames still holds the same vivid vision and emotion it did then.

Picture, if you will, where I was born, the Pacific Island paradise of Fiji, a picturesque fragment of Lemuria. Imagine golden sand, silky to the touch, a crystal-clear ocean, and proud, stately coconut trees whose fronds playfully dance in the warm breeze.

The South Pacific islands have vibrant, multi-colored flora with intoxicating fragrances. As you stroll along the coast, you can observe the luxuriant green undergrowth and untamed foliage lining the beachfront, with seaside insect life frantically going about their business.

The ocean flows uninterrupted between this Pacific paradise, with no further land mass between it and the South Pole. This is the scene of what transpires next.

With deafening screams of exhilaration, children of various ages, on their summer holidays, anticipate the next massive wave to experience the thrilling rush of body surfing.

I hadn't yet learned to swim—*oops!* Yet I refused to be left out of all that fun and excitement. *I have to be in; I have to be in there; how am I going to do this?* This was my mantra; my fear of missing out was overwhelming.

Pleading and begging with my easily manipulated aunt brought results—*yes!* She took me out in the dinghy—*yes!*

I was holding court in the dinghy, out in the unrelenting ocean, amongst my siblings and the others, giddy with an adrenaline rush, all caution thrown to the wind.

Any guesses for what comes next?

I hopped off the boat. Remember the fear of missing out?

In all the excitement, **no one noticed**. My sister was just out of reach of my right hand, so I couldn't grab her. My left arm held the dinghy.

I was thrilled and overjoyed; it felt like I was in heaven, but hang on, let's rewind a bit! Did I just say *heaven?*

In an instant, the wave yanked the dinghy out of my left hand. I was adrift, sinking, and swallowing mouthfuls of salt water. Panic, fear, and terror were my companions, as the hyper-excitement instantaneously became anguish.

Countless thoughts flooded my mind. Suddenly, every picture moved in slow motion, and the realization: *OMG! I am drowning! But I'm not ready. It's not my time.*

The more panic and fear I felt, the more I struggled.

My flailing around in the water excited my sister even more, thinking another wave was coming. My aunt was unaware of my predicament.

Realizing the futility of my situation, I ceased my struggle and surrendered, opening myself to the instant serenity, peace, love, and overwhelmingly intense white light, fully aware I was immersed in Source energy, embracing the freedom, love, and ecstasy that enfolded me. Time stopped. I was in an altered reality.

However, Source had other plans for me, and my very next memory is coughing and spluttering on the beach, saved by a young man named Herbert; he was my Earth angel. And I'm still here to tell the tale.

In hindsight, it was not my time; I had to fulfill my purpose. I had work to do as a teacher, an intuitive, and a beacon for others. This is my inner knowing.

Throughout my early adulthood, my eldest sister, Yvonne, my mentor, did her best to drag me kicking and screaming from my third-dimensional life to the multi-dimensional life I live now.

Over the years, we had many exciting adventures as we explored all things spiritual, from diving rods to past lives, healing groups to ley lines, from channeling to light language. Yvonne was the intellectual aquarian who carried deep knowledge and was a natural organizer, whereas I was the intuitive and pragmatic one; rolling up my sleeves and getting with it was my ethos! It was a synchronistic combination.

The year is 2000. Now in Sydney, Yvonne is hosting a healer from New Zealand called Colin Lambert. Colin demonstrated his healing method, which involved the healer detecting energy that needed to be cleared from the body by using his hands as the positive conduits. If the energy around the body is clear, your hands will pass over that area freely. However, if there's blocked energy, your hands stop and won't move past that blockage. That energy is solid and you need to physically lift or scoop it away from the body to remove it.

Yvonne volunteered my services to Colin and the obliging client on the massage table. *Heavens above, she's done it again!* I thought grudgingly, mumbling as I did as I was told.

I had never felt energy before and didn't think it was my forte. With Colin's guidance, the skeptic—me—couldn't explain the impact of what I was about to experience.

I felt like I had a brick wall between my hands. This was the energy that needed clearing. My hands went a deep red, and I couldn't move them, try as I might. I held the energy between my hands, my body heated up, globules of perspiration broke out on my forehead, and the energy rooted me to that spot, tingling and playing through my hands and body—not something I could dismiss!

What did I just encounter? What kind of trickery is this? It can't be true! Did this really happen?

This was my first encounter with feeling negative energy, in fact, energy of any kind. In hindsight, it was only the first time I had **consciously** connected with energy, thus starting my journey into the healing field. I felt like a child in a candy shop.

I had to have every bright bauble that came to hand; it was this searching that provided me with the knowledge and abilities I now work with.

My search magnetized me to the frequency of Dr. Joshua David Stone. He resided in Los Angeles, and I had many incredible experiences and learned infallible lessons from him, which teach in my work with my clients. While living in LA, I had the privilege of attending his Wesak festival at Mt. Shasta in 2001. It was there that I had an epiphany, which greatly expanded my multidimensional knowledge and journey.

Dr Stone is now an ascended master, so I consider myself privileged and blessed to have known him before he transitioned.

Enter Kahu Fred Sterling from The Honolulu Church of Light in Oahu, Hawaii, who was deeply entrenched in the teachings of Lemuria through the channel called Kirael. I reconnected back to my Lemuria ancestry, which I always knew, albeit unconsciously, was my primary spiritual connection. With all the searching I accomplished, this spoke to my heart and resonated deeply.

In Sydney, Australia, again, and with a group of like-minded souls, we embarked on spiritual classes and channeling and experimented with talking to the trees, an emphatically delightful experience with the tales those trees told. We cleared and worked closely with Mother Earth; these were such exciting and heady days full of experimentation and working with energy; there was nothing beyond our scope. Included in this mix was my ability to work with many clients, helping them connect to and clear past lives.

Kahu Fred decided to come to Australia and, as I worked at the longest-running esoteric bookshop belonging to the Theosophical Society, I could host him as an author. He brought some of his congregation along, and Spirit said we should go to Uluru, which is in the middle of Australia. We had work to do there regarding clearing many ancient energies. What an incredible experience that was. With Kirael's support, we set the energy for the heart of Uluru to work in harmony for the future. This interaction with Kirael brought many aha moments for me, and I will always hold Kahu Fred and Kirael close to my heart.

Come 2014, I traveled from New Zealand to the UK and spent a year in Ireland. In those emerald isles, I had time to do deep spiritual work and start my healing practice in earnest. The knowledge and practices learned through the years received major upgrades and downloads. My strong connection to spirit now enabled me to move forward with clarity. I started to work and trust my Heart Team. Today, in every moment, I feel and acknowledge their guidance and communication. They're always with me.

Clear intuition, clear knowing, and absolute trust are the culmination of all my lessons. Stepping into mastery afforded me that ability, and I now have thousands of people I work with all across the globe.

The thread woven through my personal and spiritual journey is that of the energy and essence of Lemuria. The ethos of love and wisdom was all-embracing and underlined their daily existence. My Lemurian guides work alongside me and give me the simplicity needed to manoeuvre through this incarnation, and I'm blessed beyond words. The icing on the cake was attending Ho'oponopono on the island of Hawaii with two of my sisters. The teacher was Dr. Huw Len Ihaleakala. Another synchronicity? Yes!

The important lesson from *My Story* is that I wish someone had given me a roadmap to save time. We are time-poor and living busy lives. This roadmap, if given the dedication, is a short journey to personal and spiritual fulfillment.

All inquiries on how to go in-depth are available to you below in the links.

THE PRACTICE

First off, are you super passionate and hungry to live a fulfilling life, both personally and spiritually? Are you exhausted by the unceasing upheaval, drama, and discord resulting in your daily reality?

Or are you content living a disruptive life with no desire to change?

If so, read no further. This practice isn't for you.

I don't say that lightly or mean to offend. The will to transform into a life of balance and harmony primarily needs consciousness and dedication, but it can also be so emphatically rewarding. If you're ready to leap, let's jump ahead!

Our roadmap is a well-known quote, "We're spiritual beings having a human experience" by Pierre Teilhard de Chardin.

This places importance on the spiritual us rather than the physical us. A dedicated, daily spiritual practice is the foundation needed to build upon.

Put yourself in the control seat.

Most people are unaware that energy plays such a vital role in their lives. Being conscious of your energy and keeping it clear daily undoubtedly connects you to a life in the flow of infinite possibilities and joy. If you're not in control of your energy, you'll feel your life is obstructed at every turn, and disharmony becomes your reality.

Meditation is the core of your practice. This will help build your intuition and communication skills with your guides and Heart Team. And yes, we all have them!

YOUR MEDITATION SPACE:

Choose a place you can call your own, where you can commune with your higher self, angels, guides, and other spiritual hierarchies.

This space means no cell phone; silence is mandatory, and no disruptions.

Furnish this space to reflect your intent. Remember, it's your sacred space.

Construct an altar and proudly display your sacred objects, such as candles, crystals, pictures of the Holy Family, Buddha, Quan Yin, or figurines of other sacred deities you revere.

Include a vase to hold flowers and an incense burner to cleanse non-beneficial energies from your space.

Intention is your most powerful tool, provided you intend no person, animal, or thing any harm. Intention can assist you in commanding the laws of nature to manifest your dreams and desires.

Make meditation a regular practice, daily, preferably at the same time. Start with small steps, five minutes, and increase as your intuition grows. Sitting in the quiet of your heart space, connecting with your higher self will deliver you the answers you seek. A dedicated and consistent practice will raise your vibration, frequency, and light quotient. This will help you to access and understand your gifts and begin receiving the answers you require from your spiritual team.

Follow the steps below to build a firm foundation for your roadmap.

1. CLEAR NON-BENEFICIAL ENERGIES:

Negative energies of any kind like to control and manipulate because that is their express purpose. They behave like vampires in our energy system. When they infiltrate our auric field, we experience their thoughts, feelings, and desires, giving away our power.

Benefits:

Banish negative thinking or inner voices that are critical, depressive, and suicidal.

No longer feel anxious or angry for no reason.

Headaches and migraines disappear.

No overwhelm or confusion; you are in control.

No longer be addicted to drugs, sex, alcohol, gambling, or other lower desires.

2. GROUNDING:

Grounding is mandatory on this journey. It strengthens our connection to Mother Earth, anchoring and manifesting the spiritual energies downloaded through your meditation.

When fully grounded, you know you are safe and fully empowered in your mastery.

Benefits:

Manifest your desires, intentions, and dreams

Feel strongly earthed and protected.

Your spirit is firmly anchored in the body and stays disconnected from the collective consciousness that holds others' thinking and emotions.

Releases stress, enabling peace to be your modus operandi.

3. CLEAR THOUGHT FORMS:

Your thoughts are energy that has a level of frequency. Negative thoughts create negative results and positive thoughts create positive results in your life. Your every thought interacts with the universe and is generated by your thinking. You are the creator and controller. Therefore, you create your reality.

Over time, your negative thoughts will blend into thought forms, clogging and saturating your energy field, becoming the instrument to attract even more non-beneficial energy and entities into your field.

Interacting with others through life, we inevitably connect with hundreds or thousands of people. The result is we form invisible energy cords to them and they to us. Cords are not always positive and may result in energy drainage or psychic attack from them to us or vice versa. The very act of thinking of someone enables attachment.

Benefits:

Clear all energy that is not yours from your field.

Free you up from psychic attacks and energy vampires.

Stop being drained by other's energies.

Keep vibrant and positive.

4. CHAKRAS

Regular cleansing and balancing your chakras is mandatory but is a practice often forgotten or ignored.

These seven major energy centers start at the top of your head and end at the base of your spine, influencing all parts of your mind, body, and spirit, including emotions, and helping resist disease and enhance the balance you need for harmony to thrive.

A pristine chakra system restores a harmonious flow of energy throughout your entire energy matrix, strengthening your immune system and keeping you physically and spiritually healthy.

Benefits:

Enjoy the life force flowing through the chakra column for spiritual and physical health.

Chakras invigorated for maximum well-being and vitality.

Physical organs and glands in the body are reinforced and balanced.

5. PROTECTION:

It is crucial to protect ourselves when we begin and continue this journey. After we have released all the negative energies and unwanted influences in our auric field, we need protection in place to keep our energy matrix pristine. All of the hard work you have done previously will be negated if you don't have protection in place.

The protective shield should have the flexibility to allow positive energies in and keep negative ones out.

The more you practice your protection with regularity, the stronger it will work for you and help you be a master of your energy and, therefore, be the master of your life.

Benefits:

Protection and deterrent from negative energies and entities.

Prevent the emotional energies of others entering your field.

Construct a cocoon to secure your entire pristine biofield.

Archangel Micheal is always available to call upon.

These strategies are basic practices, a foundation for you to build upon. You may have heard of divine timing. That's the essence of mastering your energy matrix. Our humanness makes us impatient to achieve what we've blocked or forgotten, with the veil of forgetfulness being responsible.

Once you start mastering your energy matrix, understand it's just the beginning. Your life will transform when you raise your vibration and merge with your I AM presence,the ultimate aim. You'll live a life filled with peace, love, and joy, with no drama or chaos.

We started with the roadmap, reminding us that 'we are spirit beings living a human experience.' Embarking and mastering these practices will achieve your personal and spiritual fulfillment.

Virginia Rounds Griffiths.

I AM a multi-dimensional light activator, energy alchemist, medical intuitive, and spiritual teacher.

My mission is to enable humanity to connect to and work within their divine heart centers. This facilitates the connection to their true essence, their own god/goddess within, empowering each soul to achieve clarity, purpose, joy, and harmony in their lives.

Einstein said, *"Everything is energy and that's all there is to it. Match the frequency of the reality you want and you cannot help but get that reality."*

The zero point field has infinite possibilities - this is the field I work in.

Most people have no idea that energy is playing such a vital role in their lives; resulting in a life lived in the flow of infinite possibilities and joy or, in a life obstructed at every turn, the result being disharmony.

I work to transform and transmute energies from negative to positive—in the environment, in personal energy fields, physical bodies, and any other areas needed, bringing balance and harmony.

My passion is to be of service to the human, animal, plant, mineral, and elemental kingdoms because when we work together, we create balance and harmony in and on our beloved Mother Earth.

Connect with Virginia:

Website: https://virginiaroundsgriffiths.com

Facebook: https://www.facebook.com/virginia.r.griffiths

Facebook: https://www.facebook.com/VirginaRoundsGriffiths/

LinkedIn:

https://www.linkedin.com/in/virginia-rounds-griffiths-384528140/

CHAPTER 19

Body Unbound

THE ART OF SOMATIC LIBERATION

Bonnie Sheldon, EFT Master Trainer, YTR500

MY STORY

I fled from the studio, the renowned choreographer's words a searing sound continuing behind me:

"You will never be a star! You are ablaze with passion! But you are not dancing the classical ballet—your extension, your arabesque! Aaaagh! You're ruining my perfect vision!"

In the solitude of the changing room, I tore away my leotard as if shedding a painful skin, no longer mine to wear. I hastily crammed my belongings into my bag, a chaotic jumble mirroring my inner turmoil. The elevator's slow arrival was unbearable; instead, I hurtled down the twelve flights of stairs, each step a descent from the world I knew.

Bursting from the building, I rounded the corner and collided with my dear friend Mark's solid sanctuary. My momentum met his sturdy frame, a grounding force amidst my disarray. "Bonnie," he asked, "what happened?"

I poured out the tale, my words tumbling over one another. With a hand as gentle as his presence was strong, Mark drew me into an embrace that spoke of new beginnings. "It's time," he murmured, "to explore a path where bodies are seen through a lens of compassion and possibility."

Guided by his steadying hand, I stepped into my first Feldenkrais class, taught by Moche Feldenkrais. On a simple mat, I found a world where movement was a dialogue, not a demand. It was the dawn of a profound transformation, where the search for perfection gave way to embracing authenticity. Once defined by rigid forms, the world unfolded with grace and acceptance. This was the beginning of a new chapter, a journey of self-discovery and change, where I learned to dance with my own unique rhythm.

As I lay on the mat, the floor beneath me felt like an extension of the Earth itself—firm, supportive, unyielding. It was a stark contrast to the wooden barres and the unforgiving mirrors of the ballet studio, where every angle of a body is scrutinized for the elusive *perfect form*. Here, the ground welcomed me without expectation.

"Let your breath be your compass," the teacher's voice was soft, a gentle current guiding me through the sea of stillness. "Inhale deeply and release a layer of effort with each exhale. Allow the earth to support you, to hold you firmly yet tenderly."

I obeyed, my body responding to the rhythm of my breath. With every inhalation, I felt my chest rise, my heart space opening. With every exhalation, I surrendered a little more to gravity, to the embrace of the ground beneath me.

"Now, invite movement like a whisper of wind through leaves," the teacher continued, his words painting a picture of grace. "Rotate your head gently, exploring the axis of your neck. There's no right angle to achieve, only the sensation to savor. Feel the weight of your skull, how the earth cradles it, how it floats atop your spine."

I moved, my head rolling slowly from side to side, not seeking but discovering, not forcing but finding.

"Let the floor be your guide," he said, his tone imbued with encouragement. "As you arch your back, press into the mat with intention, not intensity. Notice the muscles' presence; they've been quieted for so long. Listen to them; they have stories to tell."

I arched, pressing my pelvis down, feeling the muscles awaken, their voices soft yet significant. It was a conversation, not of words, but of presence, of being.

"Cease the pursuit of any goal; let curiosity become your guide." Feldenkrais' voice was now a distant melody, a lullaby for the striving spirit. "Embrace the wisdom of your form. Let your body lead, and your mind follow. Dance the dance that only you know, the one written in the language of your soul."

And so I slowly moved on the mat, finding ancient knowledge, a wisdom that needed no words, only space to be heard.

With each breath, I sank deeper into the mat's embrace, letting go of the rigidity that had once defined my movements. I was learning a new art, an embodiment that didn't require the approval of a mirror or an audience. In this space, I was not a dancer chasing perfection but simply a being moving in harmony with the earth beneath me.

This first encounter on the mat was a revelation—a gentle opening to self-acceptance and a quiet celebration of the body's unique landscape. A gentle wave washed away the rigid constructs of perfection that had long governed my dance. It was as if I was released from an invisible corset that had dictated not only my posture but also my self-worth.

My movements became more fluid and organic, no longer a series of positions to be attained but a dance of discovery, a celebration of what my body could do rather than a critique of what it couldn't. This experience was a gateway to a broader somatic journey.

My dialogue with self—awareness and gentleness on the floor led me to Rudolf Laban, whose Space Harmony work from the early 20th century was brought to the US by Irmgard Bartinieff, a newly discovered mentor and beacon who illuminated my path with her pioneering spirit.

Her teachings, which combined Laban's spatial principles with healing, wellness, and recovery, were revolutionary. "Find harmony in movement," she would say. "Let your motions be your mantra for unity and deliberate action."

The geometric beauty of movement within cubes and icosahedrons fascinated me, and I found myself reaching into the space around me, guided by Irmgard's prompts. The Bartenieff Fundamentals were no longer mere exercises but a philosophy I embraced, guiding bodily unity and intentional motion. Figures like Margaret Mead recognized her profound impact, highlighting the depth and breadth of Irmgard's influence.

"Extend beyond your edges," she said, "Your space is as vast as your imagination." With each *back-low, side-high*, and *forward-middle*, I was no longer confined by my body's borders but was expanding into the world itself. The elusive backflip, once a distant dream, now seemed within reach as I explored the uncharted territories of my backspace.

I remember trying that backflip, a movement that had long eluded me:

A moment of stillness, a deep breath in. Then, bending my knees, I push off the ground, feeling the world invert. My head guides the motion, leading the way back. It's as if my thoughts pull me through the flip, my body following the arc my mind has already traced in the air. There's a sense of surrender to the momentum, trusting that my head—my will, my intention—will bring me full circle to a steady landing. There's a rush, a blur of ceiling and ground, as I tuck my legs and rotate. For a heartbeat, I'm suspended in air, defying gravity. And then, the ground approaches, my feet reach out, and I land firmly, the thrill of the flip still tingling in my muscles.

Gratitude fills me as I reflect on the privilege of learning from such mentors whose influence reached far beyond the dance floor. "You are part of a lineage," Irmgard would remind us, "a legacy of movement that connects us all." I realized that Irmgard's teachings were not just lessons but life itself, a rhythm that beats to the pulse of our shared humanity.

My most memorable moment with Irmgard came during a session when she demonstrated the essence of Bartenieff Fundamentals. She moved with grace and vitality, and it was hard to believe she was in her late 80s. As she leaped into the air, she exclaimed, "You can fly!" Instantly, I felt a shift within me. Her words and movement unlocked something—I felt a sense of freedom and possibility I never knew before.

Her spirit lives on in me as I dance through the endless possibilities of movement and connection.

Excited by the work, I heard of other people similarly exploring movement. By this time, Thomas Hanna in California had given this a name: "Somatics," based on the Greek word "Soma" or "experience within."

Hearing that word, I knew that the new discipline could change my life; now, it could change yours. Somatics open a path to self-discovery, revealing the body as a profound tool for growth.

In the heart of New York City, I joined a cohort led by the visionary Bonnie Bainbridge Cohen. I was part of something extraordinary, a studious crew drawn together by a shared curiosity for the body's silent language. As Bonnie guided us, her words were like keys unlocking the secrets of *embodied anatomy*.

I remember thinking, *this is that very real connection between mind and body I've been searching for!* Each session was a revelation, as if our anatomy was speaking its truths, and we, the eager students, listened intently. "Notice how your body responds," Bonnie would say, her tone encouraging. "It's a conversation, not a monologue."

We worked in pairs, sometimes in threes, and the bonds formed were as real as the muscles and bones we explored. *These people get it*, I mused; the camaraderie was palpable, a shared journey into the depths of our inner construction. "You're not just learning about the body; you're learning from it," Bonnie reminded us, her words mingling with laughter and the occasional sigh of discovery.

Bonnie Bainbridge Cohen's eventual developed work, now known as Body-Mind Centering®, has since spread across the globe, touching countless lives. But back then, in those early days, it felt like we were pioneers charting unknown territories. I thought her teachings would change the world, awed by the potential that lay in her methods. And indeed, they have.

As I delved into somatic disciplines, my dance naturally began to mirror the most genuine parts of me. It was as if the chains of perfection had dissolved, liberating me to connect with the world and revel in the beauty that constantly unfolds around us.

A veil lifted, and with it, each movement I made pulsed with purpose, echoing the profound connection between my body and its every motion. This freedom infused every facet of my dance, giving me an exhilarating sense of liberation.

My heart danced too, brimming with joy; my spirit embarked on a journey of discovery, unshackled from the rigid ideals of old. The studio mirror, once a stern adjudicator, now stood as a passive observer, and the barre, once a boundary, became a steadfast ally in my dance. My performances flourished into intimate offerings of my soul's story.

This shift in perspective wove itself into the fabric of my existence. I began to see beauty in the imperfect, the transient, the real. Gazing at the autumn leaves, I remarked to my friend Mark, "Look at how they fall so gracefully, each one a fleeting dance before it touches the ground."

He nodded, "It's a reminder; nothing is permanent."

"Exactly," I replied. "And in their impermanence, there's a profound beauty. The end of one chapter, but not the story."

I smiled, watching a leaf drift slowly to the earth. *Even in their descent, there's a lesson. Each leaf tells a story of change, of letting go.*

Later, in the quiet sanctuary of my studio, I stood still, my gaze introspective.

Mindfulness, I thought, *you've become the unseen maestro of my days.* My heart echoed with gratitude for the curiosity and openness that had blossomed within me.

As I moved through the studio, my every step was a silent conversation with the world around me. "Life," I mused aloud, "is not a series of static scenes; it's vibrant, ever-changing, and rich with color."

Mark, leaning against the doorframe, watched me with a knowing smile. "You've grown," he said, his voice a soft affirmation of my journey.

I paused, reflecting on his words. "Yes, not just in years but in wisdom," I replied. "Each day is a lesson, each moment a brushstroke on the canvas of existence."

Together, we shared a look of understanding, a silent acknowledgment of the world's imperfections and captivating beauty. We were no longer speaking of a ballerina's success. In the dance of life, with its constant motion, I had found a profound tranquility—a peace that the relentless pursuit of perfection could never have offered.

So many of us have images of how we "might be." Perhaps thinner, younger, more healthy, more fit. The media drives us to think perfection is attainable with just one more diet, one more gym membership, or one more yoga class when you might not even be able to sit on the floor.

The quest for the perfect body might seem futile and often impossible to sustain. The difficulty can become an excuse for negative self-talk, leading to negative self-worth.

You don't have to carry these straining self-limitations: somatic practices are designed to help you break free from whatever might be keeping you from feeling good about yourself—feeling so good that you can go beyond what you ever thought possible in fitness, and this then expands to all of life!

Begin your journey to somatic liberation by standing before a mirror and affirming your readiness to embrace self-compassion. Gaze upon your reflection and observe your body with kindness, setting the foundation for well-being. Through this practice of somatic meditations, awaken to the harmonious unity of body, mind, and spirit.

THE PRACTICE

Embarking on the journey of self-acceptance is a personal choice, and you have the power to take the first step by delving into your body's sensations. You can control this process, a self-administered practice repeated as often as needed to become useful. If you care enough about how your body is wrapped into your mind, comfort and ease are right behind you.

Whenever you decide to engage in this practice, find a tranquil spot where you can be alone and grant yourself the time and permission to fully experience your body, emotions, and thoughts. There is no perfect time. You can complete this in 15 minutes or an hour. Work with what feels right for you.

BODY SCAN MEDITATION:

1. **Initiate Observation:** Begin at the top of your head, gently noticing any sensations without judgment.

2. **Progress Downward:** Slowly move your awareness through your body—forehead, eyes, cheeks, neck, shoulders, arms, hands, chest, abdomen, back, hips, legs, and feet.

3. **Awareness and Release:** Start again with a conscious awareness of each body part, from the forehead to the toes. As you become aware of each area, acknowledge any sensations present. Now, with intention, allow any tension to dissolve, releasing it with each breath you take.

   This process of releasing tension is a key aspect of the meditation, helping you achieve a state of relaxation and peace. This step encourages mindful recognition of your physical state, followed by a gentle letting go of any discomfort or stress. This promotes a sense of relaxation and peace throughout the meditation.

4. **Final Release:** When you reach your toes, pause for a moment, take a deep breath, and release any remaining tension or thoughts on the exhale. This final release is crucial for maintaining the relaxation and peace cultivated.

5. **Conclude the meditation with a moment of stillness** and carry this sense of calmness with you for the next step.

GRATITUDE MEDITATION—SENDING GRATITUDE TO MY BODY:

1. **Take a few deep breaths** to center yourself in this moment.

2. **Heartfelt Gratitude:**

Place both hands over your heart.

Reflect on the life-giving rhythm of your heartbeat, its ceaseless blood flow. Acknowledge the depth of emotion it cradles, and the resilience of healing it represents after heartache.

3. **Cranial Appreciation:**

Now, let's move your hands to cradle your head. Give thanks to the vessel of your incredible brain, your intricate command center, managing thought and memory, guiding you through the unseen rhythms of emotion and intuition, harmonizing the conscious with the mysterious depths of the subconscious.

4. **The Gift of Hearing:**

Touch your ears with gratitude for their ability to capture the symphony of life—from the whisper of the wind to the laughter of loved ones.

5. **Vision of Beauty:**

Rest your fingers lightly over your closed eyelids. Be grateful for your eyes, the windows that frame the world's beauty, from the simplest joys to the grandest scenes.

6. **Expression and Taste:**

Place your hands upon your mouth. Express gratitude for your voice, the conduit of thought, the delight of taste, and the simple pleasure of a smile.

7. Scent of Life:

Touch your nose, breathing in deeply. Appreciate the scents that enrich your experiences, from the fragrance of nature to the comforting aroma of home.

8. Returning to the Heart:

Bring your hands back to your heart, closing the cycle of gratitude. Thank your body as a whole for its strength, its healing, and its unwavering support.

Pause:

• Take a moment to notice how you feel.

• Breathe in peace; breathe out gratitude.

• Move on now to revisiting your body.

FINAL BODY SCAN MEDITATION:

This practice involves slowly re-scanning through your body, starting at the top of your head and moving down to your toes. Continue to silently thank each part of your body for its service and resilience. When you reach your toes, take a deep breath filled with appreciation and a sense of lightness.

CLOSING GRATITUDE MEDITATION:

"Thank you, body, for your strength and flexibility. Thank you for carrying me with grace through life's dance."

REFLECTION:

Release and gratitude intertwine, each deepening the other. Letting go eases tension and fosters a deeper appreciation for the body's resilience, softening it from within. This buoyancy lifts burdens, allowing healing and balance. Gratitude then fills the space, enhancing lightness and freedom. It's a cycle of surrender and trust in the body's wisdom, leading to a somatic awareness where gratitude is both felt and embodied.

If you'd love more work with somatics, head over to https://bonniesheldon.com and let me help you enjoy your embodiment journey as you find your ease of mind and movement!

Bonnie Sheldon, an esteemed embodiment coach and somatics specialist, has made significant contributions that have enriched the wellness and personal development landscape. Her diverse background in dance, business, and ministry has been devoted to fostering self-mastery and ease in others through mindful movement and cognitive empowerment, inspiring hope and transformation.

As a certified accredited Master EFT trainer, she teaches and mentors others, both people seeking a new career and other coaches and practitioners who desire to become certified. Her rich tapestry of experiences has endowed her with profound insights into the human psyche, which she applies to her current roles.

In her coaching practice, Sheldon addresses the critical aspects of health, physical self-compassion, and self-care. She assists individuals in finding movement ease, transcending chronic stress, releasing bodily trauma, and attaining a renewed sense of freedom and true embodiment. Renowned for her transformative capacity to aid individuals in overcoming diverse challenges, Sheldon has notably contributed to the Wounded Warrior Project, helping veterans with PTSD, and has developed programs such as Heartbreak Rescue® for women undergoing divorce or separation.

Having worked with over 9,000 clients in a lifetime of healing, she champions an embodied fitness paradigm that integrates physical activity with an acute consciousness of bodily sensations, their more profound implications, and an understanding of the mind-body connection.

Her corporate wellness work, which has unfolded in recent years, has been successful and has created a significant demand for her wellness programs in the business world.

Connect with Bonnie:

Website: https://www.bonniesheldon.com

Email: bonnie@bonniesheldon.com

LinkedIn: https://www.linkedin.com/in/bonnie-sheldon-aa38b01b0/

Facebook:

https://www.facebook.com/MindBodyIntegrationWithBonnie/

Course: https://www.transformyourexercisemindset.com

CHAPTER 20

Queen of the Intuitive Kitchen

HACKS FOR PREPPING AND MAKING GREAT MEALS EASY AND FUN

Ricki McKenna, CN, DBC

MY STORY

FIRE!

Oh no! flashed through my mind as I blurted, "Oooh, 'scuse me a sec," at the Zoom screen, grabbed a dish towel, two-stepped sideways, swiftly opened the oven door, and smothered the flames licking at the lower rack, and fortunately, visible outside the bottom of the oven.

Whew, that was one nightmare avoided.

"Hi, I'm back from smothering a fire in the oven." I shakily grinned at my cooking class audience, whose surprised faces showed a mix of astonishment then horror.

As my pounding heart returned to normal, I explained with a laugh, "Well, ladies, today's impromptu kitchen hack from RickisKitchen is how to smother a fire in your oven. It's not with water. Use a cotton kitchen towel! It seems this dish was too darn hot to handle in more ways than one." The class continues.

Prepare for a journey that's not only safer and healthier but also a heckuva lot more fun!

It's my gift to you—to encourage you into a long-lasting, healthy life of fun, ease, and joy!   With a blend of science and down-to-earth advice, we'll shatter some food myths, dish out some nifty nutritional hacks, and make picking foods and a lifestyle that treat your mind, body, and taste buds a breeze. You'll be inspired with some nutritional hacks for saving money and time, and make your kitchen a great place to hang out—as everyone usually does—where you create fabulous food easier, safer (fire-proofed), with less stress and more fun.

This part of my story began in March of 2020 when in-person networking and social gatherings were banished from public venues to working from home. The restrictions of COVID-19 presented a strange form of gift I now treasure. It challenged me to reinvent myself for the tenth or eleventh time, learn new skills and allowed me to do something I loved: play in my kitchen.

I'm a foodie with a passion for intuitively creative cooking and a mission to share the know-how.

As the world spun into chaos, my pots and pans became my saviors, and my whisks and spices, my faithful companions. Who knew that quarantine would turn me into a culinary maven, navigating the mechanisms of Zoom and the uncharted territory of homemade spanakopita?

Longing to stay active and productive and continue my nutrition business—which involves in-person meetings, counseling, and consulting—I awoke one mid-March morning with the thought: *I've been telling people for years that food is medicine. It's time to **show** them how to do it, and Zoom is the perfect medium.* Pan-Demic cooking classes were born.

These engaging, informative classes sprang from a fierce desire to provide the public with valid facts to help them navigate the pandemic and beyond. To give them a sense of real control over their health. For decades, we've been inundated with mixed and confusing messages about food and eating right. It was time to bring order to the chaos.

Remember the saying, "Do what you love, and the money will follow?" Well, my angels giggled when my fiancé excitedly agreed to my crazy plan to start a fun, educational cooking class online from our kitchen. As we chop, mince, mix, sauté, spill stuff, extinguish fires, laugh, and create simple, scrumptious dishes live on Zoom, we aim to bring clarity and joy to the table.

I'm tickled to share how my amazing *Mr. Fix-it,* Richard, who we affectionately call "the hand," a nickname he earned by sneakily reaching his hand to snatch a sample of the completed food from the chopping block so only his hand ever makes it on camera, brilliantly improvised a wooden platform nailed to a step ladder for my computer setup! With the main camera perfectly focused on our chopping block-topped island, I stand at the far end, facing the camera, and passionately demonstrate how to create miraculous meals in less than 60 minutes. We also swap ideas and tips during class time, so it's mutually beneficial, which is ideal.

A few classes later, topping his usual sparks of ingenuity, the hand connected a supplementary camera above the stove, aimed at the front burner so my audience could easily see the food cooking. I am now able to switch views as needed. Kudos to my sweetheart, the inventor.

Of course, he knew he'd get to eat all the goodies we created as a continual bonus after all his work. And at 76, I acquired yet another tech skill. Pan-demic cooking officially took off.

Six months and more than 30 classes later, I realized food and cooking are forever, pandemics aren't, thank God. *Pan-Demic* consequently morphed into *Pan-Tuitive cooking.*

And then, *There's more you have to do,* began gnawing at my brain as the classes progressed.

For years, I scribbled on pieces of paper, imagining writing a cookbook based on nutritional science, using foods, herbs, spices, and intuition, until my desktop was a confetti heap.

While the hacks and recipes were carefully filed, everything else was piled to the point of insanity. This finally induced a fury of clearing and attempts at Feng Shui-ing my office.

Somewhere between the colorful heap, the *money corner*, and the filing drawers, I knew I had accumulated valuable material for a great book.

To paraphrase Emerson, "Interesting things occur when you make a decision; the Universe hears and conspires with you to make it happen."

A bit of history: Before moving back to Houston from Aspen, Colorado, I manufactured and sold organic gourmet soups at farmers' markets and shops for several years. I gained many followers who loved the soups. Several swore, "We're losing weight eating your amazing soups."

They also began eating according to their individualized tips for healthier living and reaped the benefits from my coaching and classes. For 15 years, my healthy food and lifestyle coaching was truly making a difference for people. I realized I was on to something people wanted.

Several of my dearest clients and friends in Houston now say they are feeling more energetic and alive since modifying their diets according to my recommendations, including Richard "The Hand." I've become their favorite nutritionist. They all insisted, "You need to share this magic and publish a book!" So, with a nudge (or ten) from everyone, I finally decided to leap.

Having no clue about publishing a solo book, I followed my intuition again. That voice in my head/heart led me to consult with a couple of friends who've published several books in the same genre of healthy lifestyle, preventive medicine, food, and consciousness.

I investigated the lengthy process of organization, selecting vital nutrition information that would keep readers intrigued, sorting, creating easy, fun recipes, and choosing photos, type styles, and sizes. *Holy crap. What was I thinking? Publishing a book is a lotta work!*

"Self-doubt is one of the most insidious saboteurs of joy and success. The antidote is confidence in the unique talents and gifts life has bestowed upon you...
only a few believe in their talents enough to capitalize on them."

~ Alan Cohen

The adventure of sharing my passion with the world kept me going. There was no turning back. It was 2020. I was super motivated to continue my classes on Zoom and began organizing and outlining my first draft for a cookbook to publish on Amazon. Surprisingly, it flowed easier than I expected and launched on Amazon in March of 2021, almost exactly one year after the decision to go for it.

Amazon prints paperbacks. Ever try to keep your paperback or hardcover books open to stay flat so it's easy to read and follow recipes? Mine demanded spiral binding.

Reminder: you don't have to do it all yourself. Thanks to friends and referrals, I found a shop with the required capabilities. Upon receipt of the paperbacks, I schlep them to a wonderful local printer and have the bindings spiralized. Good idea. "The large print is easy to read, and I don't have to prop it open with soup cans!" commented the buyer for an 80-year-old, well-known Houston store as he ordered several dozen.

It's the only cookbook like it on the shelves. "I did it!"

YES, You Can Eat Well and Eat Right has been available in paperback and ebook forms (on Amazon) and in a spiral-bound version through my website since April 2021. Thus began my journey into publishing my nutrition-based cookbooks.

What does your heart secretly long for? What lights you up?

What's on your bucket list that hasn't yet been done?

A lesson confirmed at age 74: Some old phrases and cliches still hold water! And people will listen to what you say, even when they're as simple as handy kitchen hacks and tips.

Now that the books accompany me for live speaking and networking, I agree that having a published book gives a speaker more credibility. I can help more people.

As one happy follower commented about my book,

> "…even though I have been cooking and baking for a long time,
> I found many valuable hints and tips
> I will incorporate into my cooking."
>
> ~ S. Miles

My point; life continues with more confidence, and I grow daily. I've celebrated a few more birthdays, led more online classes, and gathered some sharable wisdom along the way.

From a dear friend and collaborator, I have learned,

"Self-care is giving the world the best of you -
not what's left of you."
~ Mari Geist

A brilliant reminder for us all.

THE PRACTICE

Good hacks for your kitchen safety (self-care) and healthful lifestyle choices:

- Freeze lemon and orange zest in tightly closed glass jars for quick access and easy use.

- Use a good veggie wash for all veggies and fruits, even bananas that share the fruit bowl, as soon as you get them home. Reason: all those hands and sneezes from the market may have left residues besides the chemicals and packing materials on your food.

- For safe and lasting storage, spin or towel dry all your leafy greens after washing (lettuce spinners are great), and store them wrapped lightly in paper towels or lint-less dish towels, then in green storage bags*.

Get *Green Bags which are available in supermarkets and online. Your food will last longer, and you'll save time and money and your greens won't wilt before you can eat 'em.

- Sharp knives matter! Learn to sharpen (find a YouTube video) or have them sharpened often as needed, so you can easily slice tomato skins*; saves slipping and cutting fingers.

*Tomato skins can be tough, especially when ripe; your sharp knife should cut them easily.

- Use the correct knife for the job. Paring knives are great for small foods, larger ones for meats, and larger, tougher vegetables like carrots, parsnips, beets, etc. Choose the knives with which you are comfortable and work best for the job.

- Wash all can tops with soap and water before opening. Who knows what critters crawled on them while transporting them or in the back store room?

- Wash your spice jars and bottles frequently. They get sticky and transfer bacteria.

- Chiffonade* leafy greens like Swiss chard, spinach, and basil for easy cooking and garnishes. *How: Stack the leaves, roll tightly, and slice perpendicular to the roll. Good for soups and crepes, too.

- Smash individual garlic cloves gently with the flat side of a chef's knife to easily peel.

- Refrigerate freshly peeled, ready-to-use garlic in a glass jar with a double layer of plastic wrap under the jar top. Saves the refrigerator from smelling like garlic.

- Read labels on **everything** that's in a package: in food jars, boxes, plastic bags, even wine. If there are ingredients you don't recognize, look them up with your phone or call me. Know that there *are* some safe packaged foods, like fermented foods, organic butter, freshly packed raw non-GMO vegetables and fruits, and more.

- Over 24 different sugar substitutes are available from various sources and ingredients. Some are safe, and some are not. Be careful of your choices—check the internet or call me.

- For cleaning fruits and vegetables, I recommend Truly Free* Fruit and Vegetable Wash. It's economical and can be refilled, which cuts down on repetitive plastic bottles. Available on my website under "Recommendations" or online.

After serving a variety of people for the past 24 years, their needs, bodies, circumstances, and connections to food, I have learned more than a few facts about living well with joy and staying free from disease. I hungrily research a lot!

Remember, we are each a unique child of the Universe, biochemically, physically, and psychologically. Therefore, when you eat well and eat right for *your body*, consciously choose a healthy lifestyle that works for you, you and your family will have better chances of achieving and maintaining healthy lives *with food as your medicine.*

Disclaimer: The purpose of this chapter is not to diagnose, cure, or in any way prescribe or give medical advice. These statements are for informational purposes only. The content is not intended to be a substitute for professional medical advice, diagnosis, or treatment. Always seek the advice of your physician or other qualified health provider with any questions you may have regarding a medical condition or prescription. Never disregard professional medical advice or delay in seeking it because of something you read in this chapter.

SEVERAL NUTRITIONAL MYTHS AND TRUTHS:

Myth 1. Organic foods are not affordable on a budget.

Truth: Organic foods can help prevent disease since they are grown without using commercial fertilizers, pesticides, and herbicides that may interrupt your body's natural processes. Reduce sensitivities/allergies and doctor bills, and eat "cleaner" food.

Myth 2. Tap water everywhere is safe to drink.

Truth: To know for certain what is in your tap water and where it comes from, contact your local water utility. The Environmental Protection Agency (EPA) requires all water suppliers to issue an annual report to their customers called a Consumer Confidence Report. Learn more: Look for your water report on the EPA's local drinking water information page at www.epa.gov/safewater/dwinfo/index.html. If you're not sure, invest in a good filter for your kitchen for drinking and cooking. They are effective, cost less than plastic bottled water, and you'll not clog the environment with more plastic as well.

Myth 3. Carbohydrates are bad for you.

Truth: Your body needs good carbs. The complex ones from vegetables and fruits provide energy along with a balance of proteins and fats. Foods like baked goods and fried foods are not the best. Choose fruits and veggies, nuts and seeds. Add an egg (protein and fats) to your oatmeal (carbs) to get more lasting energy from your breakfast.

Myth 4. Food doesn't need to be colorful or attractive - it's just food.

Truth: We eat first with our eyes. Adding color to your meals brings your senses into the experience. Your eyes get to participate and enjoy food (almost) as much as your mouth does. The bonus is the variety of colors and foods bring you different vitamins, minerals, and phytonutrients your body wants and needs. This also helps prevent disease.

Myth 5. Food can't prevent disease.

Truth: Yes, it can! Here is one example; "Fish and seafood are excellent lean protein sources without any of the saturated fats of meat. Introducing more seafood into your diet may yield numerous health and nutrition benefits. Seafood is also better than meat as it lowers the risks of heart disease, stroke, and several cancers associated with consuming meat." (WebMD)

With a shopping basket full of self-care, confidence, the support of friends and family, and my perpetual quest for understanding leading the way, I hope I've given you some concepts, ideas, and positive arguments for eating consciously and with thoughtful planning. Listen for your still-small (sometimes screaming) inner voice. It's the truth you can always trust.

Here's to your healthy lifestyle and hearty appetite.

Hi. I'm **Ricki Mckenna**, CN, DBC, a certified nutritionist and Dream Builder coach, chef, show host, speaker, best-selling author, and grandma. I love people, and preparing and then sharing food. For more than 25 years, I have empowered individuals and families to create and experience radically healthier, richer, more productive, and joy-filled lives with food.

I **know** that food is the key to healthy living and longevity. Food is medicine.

As a founding member of The Holistic Center for Human Flourishing in Carbondale, Colorado. I began speaking about health and nutrition to the public in 2001 and writing a weekly column for the Aspen Daily News. I'm a long-time member of the National Association of Nutritional Professionals, Zonta Club International, and The Wellness Universe, where we're making the world a better place, through our holistic wellness work. I love speaking and am available to create food demonstrations for your organization.

My newest book, *YES You Can Eat Well and Eat Right, and Find the Joy of Cooking*, is available on Amazon. The spiral-bound version, which is more practical, is available at a discount from my website, Rickiskitchen.net.

A Long Island, New York native, I've also lived in the Rocky Mountains of Colorado and now call Houston, Texas, home. My favorite place is the Rocky Mountains, where I find peace and inspiration for my life. Seventy-nine years of living, with over 25 years professionally coaching women and men desiring to create healthier lifestyles, have given me diverse experiences that inspire my writing, speaking, and consulting. I love bringing nutritious, delicious, and healthy together.

For a free copy of my ebook, call me and mention this chapter at 970-618-7607.

I will answer the phone!

Connect with Ricki:

Ricki@RickisKitchen.net

Ricki@Rickimckenna.com

Website: https://RickisKitchen.net

For recipes and blogs and a free ebook*, go to

https://patreon.com/rickiskitchen

thewellnessuniverse.com/world-changers/rickimckenna

Find me on Facebook: https://www.facebook.com/rickiskitchen/

CHAPTER 21

When You're Shattered

CREATING WONDER AND MAGIC FROM THE PIECES

Star Studonivic

MY STORY

On this day, I returned empty-handed from the hospital. I should've had the soft bundle of my already-cherished child cradled in my welcoming arms. He died. So did my husband. So did my life.

Why am I left behind, and why am I still here?

Embers softly illuminated the rim of my wineglass—a circle of light. Catching the rich garnet tones of the remaining wine, I swirled the glass and raised it to the heavens. *Divine Being, help me want to live because I don't. I want to die, go away, go to sleep, and never wake up. I can't do this. If you're there, help me. I beg you.*

My toast completed, I downed the remains, doubting my pleas were heard. Replacing the glass on the polished table, I watched as the final sparks of a dying fire leapt upwards, only to be met with the resistance of gravity to plummet and die.

My emotions matched their descent. Leaning into the comfort of a soft throw, I clutched it to my heart in desperation. From the deepest, primal part of my being, I witnessed my scream rip the calm. **"Nooooo.**

Nooooo. I can't." There was a second of silence, followed by the shattering of the crystal wineglass. I watched as if I was a disembodied ghost as the shards scattered across the table, tumbling to the floor and hearth—a discordant symphony.

A gust of wind rattled the window. Still clutching the throw in my quest for comfort, I watched the frenzied dance of cotton candy snowflakes.

Why are the freezing gusts moving the flakes through my window? They're creeping into my heart; I'm numb. I can't hear. As the chill continued through me, it spread like a deadly virus.

I can't feel my heartbeat. Is this what it's like to have a frozen heart? Maybe my plea was heard. Am I dying? Eerie calm enveloped me. I watched the remaining pieces slide to their final resting place. Utter hopelessness assumed residence within. *Nothing matters. Not anymore. Will it ever?*

Death, desertion, betrayal, and desperation wove into a tight bundle and settled in my stomach. Not easily digested. The quicksand of despair strangled every breath. Shallow, timid breath seemed all I was deserving of. *How little space can I occupy? How can I just simply disappear and not matter?* I closed my eyes. *Maybe I can just dissolve. Go away. Anywhere. Finally end this journey. Why am I still breathing?*

The window panes shivered. Moonlight dared to peer through the baren bush barely visible in the darkness. Its feeble, thin branches made hesitant scratching sounds timed with intermittent gusts of wind. The branches were as bare as my soul. I was empty.

The ancient grandfather clock chimed nine. Each chime spoke of doom.

Another sound accompanied the chime. *Why would someone be ringing my doorbell this time of night? In the middle of a snowstorm?*

The doorbell chimed again. An annoying intrusion.

Not bothering to turn on a light, I slowly walked toward the door.

"Who's there?" I queried.

No reply. Looking through the peephole revealed nothing. Curiosity overcame hesitation as I slowly opened the door. Unexpected bright moonlight shone a spotlight on a basket covered with a pink blanket.

Oh my God! Did someone leave a baby at my doorstep?

I panicked. There were no signs of anyone. None. A soft "meow" interrupted my panic. There was a packed bag beside the basket. The pink blanket moved aside, directed by a tiny grey paw. Big blue eyes peered into mine. Dumbfounded, I grabbed the basket and bag, quickly deposited both inside the entryway and slammed the door behind me. Chilled and shaking, I knelt beside the basket. Blue eyes maintained a steady gaze as a grey-striped head emerged from the blanket. I reached for this tiny bundle and held it close to me. Thinking the pink blanket was indicative of this little one's sex, I wrapped her inside my bathrobe close to me. I was rewarded with a soft purr and nuzzle.

The warmth of a loving tiny kitten shattered me. Cradling this precious bundle, I lay on the floor clutching her as if my life depended upon her and sobbed.

THE PRACTICE

Shards—the pieces of our lives. Sometimes, they shatter into fragments that seem impossible to reassemble. They aren't. Each piece holds a lesson, an emotion, wisdom, a path, a hope, and a dream. What's important is how you put the pieces together. What's the picture you want? How can you change it? Do you want to change it? Is it in your best interest to change it? Is it a mosaic set in stone or in sand, easily shifted?

Or are you a kaleidoscope—beautiful pieces constantly shifting into intricate designs? All of us carry myriad possibilities. As many as there are stars in the sky.

Life teaches us the substance holding the pieces together is as important as the pieces themselves. Do you set your shards deeply into rigidity? Do you prefer a softer substance that allows for mobility? Do you embrace change or resist it? Are your beliefs stiff and unyielding? Do your shards line up into straight, linear lines or take a meandering path? What about the colors? Do they harmonize? What about texture and form?

You're both artist and director. Your choices move the pieces of the magnificent work of art that's you. You can build a monument worthy of respect. Or you can cover the pieces in mud and watch them harden and crumble while you sit on a curb and pout. It's your choice.

THE ART OF YOU

The art of you is softening the edges of each piece, both joyous and sad, and placing them where they'll be the most powerful to guide you and others. You can change your picture at any time. Refine it. Sharpen the focus. Or you can decide upon an entirely different path, throw all the pieces into the air, and see where they land. All these actions depend upon what you want to create.

Each of us enters this life with our own bag of shards. What we do with them and how we place them matters. We matter. Even if your life has been difficult, there's always room for hope, joy, and gratitude for the good things. Reach out, snatch those pieces, and place them gently within your heart. Be aware of how each piece shapes you, your emotions, and your beliefs. Challenge yourself to take the road less traveled. Inhale gently and risk forging an unknown path, trusting you'll arrive at the destination best for you. No matter how dire your circumstances, there's one certain fact. Your life will change. It can change. And you can make it happen.

The soft pieces awaken your vulnerability, which is true strength. They allow you to be your best human. Permit yourself to feel every feeling. No fair shunning the ones you don't like. Sometimes, those are the ones from which we learn the most. Life can be a full range of experiences. Notice what you learn from all your pieces.

HOW?

How? Where's the owner's manual and instructions? Ahhh. That's where we listen to our dreams, hopes, and desires. Allow them to shape your artwork. No matter how lofty the dream is, it can come to fruition. The trick is belief. Believe in yourself and believe in something greater than you. Call it the Divine.

In those brief moments between sleep and wakefulness, theta brain waves are your connection to something greater. This something allows dreams to hold the possibility of manifestation! This magical slice of time reminds us of our connection to the Divine as well as the sliver of the divine within and is the secret of connection with all. After all, we're made of many elements, including stardust. We're not separate. We're part of everything and everyone in the universe. We're the ones who pull the veil of invisibility around us (acknowledging that it's sometimes a safe place to stay for a brief period of time). We're the ones who hide in the realm of separation.

Sometimes throughout life, we feel separated from the Divine, or Higher Power, or whatever name you give your belief. In retrospect, it's *us* who create separation and isolation. We share this planet. We share and breathe the same air. Like it or not, there isn't separation.

And what are all these things: the air, the earth, the water? Many believe it's a manifestation of the Divine, who nourishes us in every way. We can refuse this nourishment, but eventually, without nourishment, there's death. Look around you and notice those who exist rather than live. A big difference: existing is a slow death. Why not acknowledge what's causing your feelings of isolation, shine a light on the core issue or issues, and discover reconnection?

How? Pull yourself out of your thinking mind and place your hands on your heart. Sit quietly, preferably outside. Every beat of your heart is life. Every breath is connection. Don't think. Feel. Breathe. Place your feet (barefoot if possible) upon the ground. There's firmness in this action. Stability, safety, and home. There's support. Stand up and feel the earth beneath you as you move. It's called grounding. It feels good. It's plugging yourself back into the circuitry of life. It's connecting you to your environment. It's where you live.

Continue your walk. Touch a leaf. Your skin and nerves feel the texture. Your eyes see the shapes and colors. What about your sense of smell? With your hand still gently upon the leaf, close your eyes. There's still a connection even though you can't see the leaf. Acknowledge what you can't see. Tune into what you feel in the deepest center of your being. Sometimes, we shut our eyes to what's around us. It doesn't mean these things have gone; we've just shut our eyes. Everything's still there. It didn't leave you. You simply closed one of your senses. The art of life is fully embracing and using every sense.

Listen with your heart as well as your ears. Give yourself permission to be. The wind carries messages. So does the smile of a baby. Allow yourself to be fully present and aware. Tune in to yourself as well as the world around you. Pay attention. Nourish the connections. Engage and participate. Every moment is both precious and informative. We've been given this gift of life. Unwrap yours and live it. You have an opportunity to live yours to your fullest. Choices again: exist or live.

NOTICE THE SMALL THINGS

Notice the small things, the ones so minute they seem insignificant. Sometimes, they create a tsunami of change within when they awaken your sense of wonder. Look as if through the eyes of a child. Be amazed at the beauty in which you're surrounded. Listen to the sounds, the pulse of life around you and within you. The feeling of air kissing your skin. The freshness of summer rain. Inhale all the scents. Touch the earth and water. Allow yourself to absorb wonder. Let those feelings permeate your being. Wiggle your barefoot toes in morning dew-kissed grass. Be fully present for each and every moment.

Find your sense of play. When was the last time you skipped down a street? Or down the aisle of the grocery store? There's muscle memory. Yes, it's a thing. You actually have brain cells throughout your body, not just in your brain. Trust you'll remember how to do this. Don't think about how it looks or what people might think. Who knows? They might feel your contagious joy and join you. At the very least, they'll smile. When was the last time you whistled to the tune playing in your head? When was the last time you became a rock star in your car? Blast that music and sing out loud. At the top of your lungs. With passion and gusto.

A favorite memory: my ancient but well-cared-for shiny red Fiat 124 Spider convertible is at a dead stop in traffic. Top's down. Squinting as bright, warm sun tingles my skin, I gaze ahead at the long snake of rush hour traffic. Exhaust fumes rev up to a crescendo in the horrid, dense traffic and settle in wafts of toxic air. My very favorite aria from Tosca, "Vissi d'arte" (I live for art), is blaring loud enough to be heard for half a mile. It's competing with the reverberating sounds of hard rock several lanes to my left. I crank the volume. Opera vs rock. Rock has more base, but I have better speakers. They vibrate with Tosca's passionate words. *Yes! I do live for art.* Her words resonate within my soul as I match my voice to hers. Devoid of breath as passion spent and the aria ends, I pause.

Where's the applause coming from? I swear I heard it. Oh my God! It's from the car next to me. They think it's me singing! Wow. I'm good. No, I'm great.

For three minutes, I became Maria Callas. Mustering a dignified nod of my head in acknowledgement of appreciation, I stepped on the accelerator as the light turned green.

Invite another soft, nourishing breath all the way down to your relaxed belly bowl. Discard the veil of invisibility. You don't need it. Stand in your power and humbleness. Tear down the wall of separation. It doesn't serve you. Acknowledge who and what you are and strip away the fear preventing you from being your best masterpiece. You're meant to be here. You belong. Everything you need is within. And you are enough. You can do this. Will you?

And as a reminder of how you place your shards, I'll leave you with this quote from Laura Jean Truman:

> *"Keep my anger from becoming meanness.*
> *Keep my sorrow from collapsing into self-pity.*
> *Keep my heart soft enough to keep breaking.*
> *Keep my anger turned toward justice, not cruelty.*
> *Remind me that all of this,*
> *Every bit of it,*
> *Is for love.*
> *Keep me fiercely kind."*

Star Studonivic is a Reiki Master and certified Yoga instructor. Her yoga specialties are primal movement (which can be done seated), seated yoga, restorative yoga, and basic fundamental yoga. Her classes are particularly designed for those who are movement-challenged. Primal movement is based upon Annie Adamson's Primal Vinyasa (https://primalvinyasayoga.com).

Star's most humbling experience (and there have been many) was with a student who is a wheelchair-bound quadriplegic whose reason for attending class was simply because class enabled her to breathe easier and know she was part of a community and accepted. She taught the entire class about connection.

Star also uses tuning forks, essential oils and crystals to assist with Reiki sessions as well as ritual work. Her ritual work is tailored to the needs of her client. She is also a calligrapher and artist. One of her calligraphic offerings is ancestor messages.

A lifelong interest and study in maintaining optimum good health led to becoming a distributor of completely natural health-enhancing products.

Connect with Star:

Website: https://www.studonivic.com

Email (Including ancestor messages): studonivic@gmail.com

Natural health support: https://Avinihealth.com/studonivic

CHAPTER 22

It Wasn't Your Fault

A PREFACE TO A POSSIBLY POSITIVE LIFE FOR TRAUMA SURVIVORS

Rev. Michol Mae, MSc

MY STORY

"Everything that surrounds you right now in your life, including the things you're complaining about, you've attracted. Now, I know at first blush that is going to be something you hate to hear. You're going to immediately say I didn't attract the car accident; I didn't attract this particular client, I didn't particularly attract the debt, I didn't attract whatever it happens to be that you are complaining about. And I'm here to be a little bit in your face and to say yes, you did attract it. And this is one of the hardest concepts to get, but once you've accepted it, it's life-transforming. This is part of the overall giant secret here."

I paused the movie *The Secret* while the words hit me like fists.

Is it my fault that I was abused as a child? Is it my fault that I had terrible, unhealthy relationships as a teen? Is it my fault I was assaulted physically, emotionally, and sexually? Is it my fault I didn't have parents as a teen?

My fingers hovered over the pause button of the remote indecisively.

I see the value of the law of attraction; it's like what my grandmother was teaching me, but those who've been victims of abuse from a young age might shut down hearing this.

"The Universe likes action. You can't just think positive; you start with thinking positive, then you feel positive, then take positive steps," I could hear my grandmother's words.

I was a teen sitting on the couch in front of the coffee table as I watched my grandmother rock back and forth in her sliding chair. The sun poured into the window behind her creating a halo effect, an angelic appearance. I looked up from her long house dress, to where her nose would've been (if not for the cancer) and returned her smile.

Grandma always tells me to think positive and positive things will happen. Even after everything she has gone through.

"If you think positive, positive things will come," my grandmother repeated.

"So just think good things, and they will happen?" My tone was dubious.

My grandmother smiled from ear to ear as she looked at me: ash blonde hair rebelliously covering half my face.

"It's not just about thinking positive. If you think positively, you start to pay attention to it, you start to feel it, and you start to act on it. I know more than you think. We have the gift of sight in this family. It comes from our heritage; we are Blackfoot Sioux, and we must honor that heritage."

I smiled. *She's really proud; she says that almost every time I visit.*

As I looked at the golden Asian city encased in a red eye-shaped translucent container backed by a mirror, my grandmother followed my gaze.

"I brought that back with me when I went to Taiwan to claim the body of your uncle from the Vietnam War; he wasn't much older than you are now."

I sat, listening, looking around my grandmother's cluttered living room, absorbing her wisdom. There were gifts from people she married (or offered other ceremonies to) in every spare space of the room. I saw a few cards addressed to her name prefaced with Reverend.

Is there space left for anything else?

My eyes glanced over to a few more figurines from Taiwan, one encased in glass and mirror and others standing tall with flowers from their backs.

"I was homeless when I met your grandfather, you know?" My grandmother's voice broke into my thoughts.

"I know, Grandma," I said with a smile.

"He was a great horse trainer and a fighter. We rode the trains together because we didn't have a home. He came straight off the boat with his sisters."

She's traveled so far and survived so much.

"I'm telling you, I've gone from homeless to having everything I need or want. Just try it; if you think positive, positive things will happen. You, my granddaughter, can do anything you put your mind to."

I feel like she sees me and believes in me.

My memories skipped ten years ahead; I was a young woman in sociology class looking out the window as I heard the instructor say, "Society often blames the victim because it's easier; there's no action that needs to be taken if it's the victim's fault."

Well, isn't that something? Is that why my father didn't believe me when I was thirteen? Was it easier? Is that why no one took any of the attacks seriously?

I replayed an old scene while staring out the window in class.

I stumbled from the cemetery, tears streaking down my face, mixing with blood. I saw the door to the shoe repair shop. Everyone on the street seemed to stare at me in horror.

Liv opened the door and hurried me inside. "What happened to you!?

"They jumped me."

"Here, sit on the counter, let me help clean you up. Do you want to see your face?"

I shook my head "no" slowly.

Liv delicately tended to my face and wounds before taking me to a mirror. My hair had blood smeared in places that gentle dabs couldn't clean, and my face held a residue of dirt and blood; my lips were swollen.

Liv held me for a few moments before I left to return home.

"Wake up!"

I jolted my head up from the kitchen table, irritated.

"I've called your father. He will be here soon to take you to the hospital."

"I just need to take a nap."

"You can't nap after a head injury! Wake up!"

Searing white filled my vision every time I came close to the promise of sliding into that pleasant darkness of sleep.

They wheeled me into the ER to a room made up of curtains. "She has a concussion, a severely bruised nose, possibly a hairline fracture, bruising throughout, but overall, she's very lucky that she didn't have much worse."

Why didn't I know better than to trust him?

As the memory faded, I found myself outside the college counselor's office. *It doesn't look as dingy as the counselor's offices in middle school and high school did.*

"How are we doing today?"

"In class, they were talking about blaming the victim, and it brought up some bad memories. A lot of them."

"Why don't you try writing about it? Perhaps a letter to yourself about what you remembered."

My middle school counselor gave me a journal and suggested I write. I'd forgotten about that until now.

A Poetic Letter to My Childhood Self

You deserved to be a child, to laugh and to play,

You deserved to always, and I mean *always*, be safe.

It's not your fault that men, with their twisted and perverted ways,

Crossed boundaries and worse while telling you it was just play.

You didn't ask for any of the things that happened to you,

Nor were you responsible for their actions towards you,

It was not because "you're so pretty" or "such a good girl,"

It was because of broken men in a broken world.

You became a caretaker and housecleaner, expected to get perfect grades,

Playtime became less and less as grown-up tasks filled your days,

It wasn't your fault they asked so much of you so young,

You deserved to be out with others your age, laughing and having fun.

It wasn't your fault when you found yourself alone with that older guy,

Going from such a strict household to one that left you to your own devices,

You deserved to be protected from this kind of danger,

Regardless of how you dress or even flirty behavior.

Had they taken the time to understand the trauma of your past,

Or simply how different your brain was wired from the rest,

They may have seen that you saw your behavior as being nice,

Not an invitation to indulge in someone else's vice.

It wasn't your fault they saw you as an adult when you were a child,

Or that they couldn't face the skeletons in the closet and stayed in denial,

You didn't wish for any of this, encourage it, or make it happen,

What you needed and deserved was protection and compassion.

It's not your fault that your mom passed from this world to the next,

I know you think you could have healed her, could have helped her rest,

If only you'd gone back home, you could take care of her again,

And she'd still be here, and perhaps it would ease all your discontent.

I know you were desperate for love and very naive,

You didn't deserve to be treated badly or beat.

It wasn't your fault, your brain wasn't developed completely,

You chose the wrong people and gave your love too freely.

The truth is you deserved to be protected and cared for,

And you deserved to be loved even more.

It feels good to write to myself, to acknowledge what I have survived.

As I was working one day in the campus library, my pocket vibrated. I unfolded the phone and answered.

"Your grandmother has passed," came the voice on the other end.

I closed my phone slowly and moved to a quiet space to sit. *Think positive and positive things will come. Is this something I can test to honor her and her legacy, and our heritage?*

I sat down with a paper and pen as if I was about to tackle a new assignment.

I wrote:

Step One: Awareness. Become aware of my thoughts.

Step Two: Acknowledge the negative day-to-day thoughts.

Step Three: Look for benefits or positives for each negative.

Step Four: Continue being aware and active even in a stressful situation.

Step Five: Practice self-compassion

The first challenge to the experiment came when my metallic green Chevy Nova refused to move. It sat in front of my Victorian house with the hood up, as I wiped the grease on my jeans. *Great, more stress, another thing to go wrong, and, of course, another thing to pay for. I can't afford this! How will I get to work and school?*

Step One: Be Aware of the thoughts. Step Two: Acknowledge the thoughts: they were negative. Step Three: Look for positives. At least we were not driving when it broke down. It's right out front. You didn't need to have it towed.

"Excuse me, do you need help?" I watched my neighbor emerge from next door.

"I've tried troubleshooting everything that makes sense, but…"

He smiled, "I'm a mechanic; let me take a look."

Wow, that was fast; I tried to correct my thoughts, and now here is a mechanic.

Maybe there's some truth to this.

Step Four: Continue to practice.

Some years later, as I sat on my blue porch by the blue door of my new home that symbolized my departed cousin. A book called *The 4 Agreements*, previously plucked from the self-help shelves of my sanctuary bookstore, sat finished on my lap.

Grandma would have given me this same advice. Instead of 'Be impeccable with your word,' she would say, 'Be true to your word.' Instead of, 'Don't make assumptions,' she would say, 'You know what they say when you assume.' Instead of 'Don't Take things Personally,' she'd say, 'Don't worry about what others say.'

And she'd agree to always do your best. It's like having her here with me again for a little while.

A Poetic Letter to Myself,

I know you think you'll be all grown up the second you hit eighteen,

But by the time you're thirty, you'll realize you were still in between,

Still growing and learning, and changing your mind with ease,

So certain you had all the answers, offering your expertise.

I'm sorry that you didn't have a dad to show you how you should be loved,

It wasn't your fault you kept picking the wrong guys unable to accurately judge,

Convinced you could fill the void in your heart by giving them more love,

Unable to see that the more you gave, the more damage they wrought.

It wasn't your fault when someone you trusted kept pouring drinks,

And someone slipped something in one making it hard to think,

I know the violation that you felt led to an oppressive darkness,

That could have cost you your life, but it saved it instead.

I think it is amazing that you keep getting up every day and dreaming,

Refusing to give up, working hard, and searching for life's meaning.

You can't save or help everyone, I know you can't help but try,

Most of the time it led to pain, heartache, and sacrifice,

I know you question if the decisions you made were right,

But those decisions are already made so it couldn't be anything else.

Pain comes from too much focus on the past or the future,

If you could have done more you would have, nothing is truer,

You've had plenty of compassion for everyone else,

Now it's time to cultivate self-compassion for yourself.

It's interesting, looking back, realizing I was still a child but held myself to adult standards. I demanded perfection, and every mistake felt catastrophic.

I understood it then. *The Law of Attraction* is not passively sitting back and dreaming; it's getting clear on your vision, leaning into it, feeling it deeply, and acting towards what you want.

A decade or so later, someone told me. "Happiness is a choice" as I struggled with the most difficult and tragic loss of my life.

I was furious. It's been two months since Jonny passed. I'll never feel joy again. How could I?

Still, the words niggled me. Life is a series of choices. I applied everything I learned from my grandmother and the many books that helped me before. I chose to heal. Healing wasn't easy, but it was worth it, and I continue to apply my grandmother's wisdom.

THE PRACTICE

Numerous studies show the benefits of meditation, visualization, and art therapy. I use these to process emotions, thoughts, and dreams. While audio is not necessary, you can find supporting audio and other materials here: https://www.ladymaeimpressions.com/GiftsOfWisdom.

Automatic or free writing is uncensored, unedited, raw writing. Allow the words to come through without judgment and flow onto the page or the computer. There's no right or wrong as long as you keep writing. I found a timer is helpful for these exercises.

A vision board is another tool that can help you get clear on your goals, desires, and dreams. You don't need to be an artist, and nothing needs to be perfect.

PHASE 1: PREPARATION

- Grab something to write or type with.
- Grab a timer (most phones have them).
- Grab poster board.
- Grab markers, colored pencils, or crayons.
- Get comfortable (I like to put the fireplace on the TV and light some candles).

PHASE 2: VISUALIZATION: CURIOUS AWARENESS OF YOUR MIND

Close your eyes and allow your mind to drift. Be aware of each thought that floats through your mind. Is it positive? Is it negative? How does it make you feel? Be curious. Where does this thought come from? How old is this thought?

PHASE 3: WRITE! SET A TIMER FOR FIVE MINUTES

On a blank sheet of paper, create three columns labeled Positive, Negative, and Neutral (or get a template from my website). Write everything that came to mind in one of the three columns as fast as you can. If your mind wanders, that's okay; write down those thoughts, too!

PHASE 4: REFRAME, COMPARE, AND CONTRAST

Without self-judgement, from a place of curiosity and self-compassion, take a few moments to read through your columns.

Choose something(s) from one of the columns, and on a separate piece of paper, write everything that comes to mind. How does it make you feel? Be curious. Where does this thought come from? How old is this thought?

PHASE 5: VISUALIZATION: A LITTLE FUN WITH YOUR DREAMS

Imagine your best life. How would it look? What would be important to you? Imagine what that life would smell like, feel like, and look like if it was the life of your dreams. How does this new life make you feel?

PHASE 6: DRAW!

If you don't want/like to draw you can also print out pictures of things that represent your best life. Set a timer for five minutes.

On your poster board, write/draw/paint/sketch, or glue representations of your goals, dreams, and visions. The goal is not perfection. It's getting your goals onto the page.

PHASE 7: SELF-COMPASSION!

Write yourself a letter. For each of the negatives on your list. Imagine if your child or best friend said them to you; what would you say to them? What advice would you give?

You can do these exercises any time for one goal or many to help with positive thinking or bring awareness to your thoughts.

Michol Mae is the founder of Lady Mae Impressions, bestselling author, award-winning poet, educator, renegade artist, and musician. An intuitive, she weaves wisdom, experiences, meditation, shamanism, sound, energy healing, and her many crafts into her programs, poetry, music, and novels.

Her mission is to bring awareness to emotional intelligence, suicide, and mental health by encouraging creativity and curiosity as necessary tools for the toolbox. She shares her journey openly, hoping it helps others avoid mistakes and heartache or heal that which couldn't be avoided.

Michol loves all furry friends, and you'll find her cats, Mac Lir and Cheeky Neeky, on her social media. In her "spare" time, you can find her writing, riding her motorcycle, spending time in nature, and practicing her many crafts. She shares the tools she uses to heal and find peace on the path to joy.

Connect with Michol:

Website: https://www.ladymaeimpressions.com

https://linktr.ee/ladymaeimpressions

Epilogue: Embracing Inner Wisdom

I can't remember reading a book of this type—ever—that touched me so deeply as this one did. The practices described here are amazing and powerful in their own right, but for me, the real *Gifts of Wisdom* reside in the remarkable stories that my dear friends have written with such tenderness within these pages.

When I finished reading, I experienced what I can only describe as a kind of *buzzing* energy.

Not the buzzing of a chaotic wasp's nest.

Not the buzzing of a high-powered electrical line.

Not the buzzing of a torn speaker in a stereo system.

No, I'm talking about the intense buzzing of the high-frequency vibration of my inner essence—a deep part of me pulsing with a profound sense of purpose that transcends description. I suppose I'm talking about the buzzing of *Bliss*. Perhaps you noticed something like this yourself.

Breath.

Movement.

Joy.

Humor.

Vulnerability.

Open hearts.

These are some common elements and themes I experienced as I read these wonderful pages. Frankly, I'm blown away by the depths to which each author dived to bring you such beautiful and insightful wisdom. But there are a couple of other ideas that arose in my awareness as well:

1. **Magnificence**—or what I prefer to call *MagnifEssence*. Deep down, this is what we all are. And if you love yourself enough to engage in the practices these authors have shared with you, you will surely find your way to connect to that ineffable quality within yourself.

2. **Resonance**. There is truth in this book. And I really mean *Truth*. Yes, with a capital "T." If you allow yourself to open to the fullness of each author's offering, I'm sure you'll feel it yourself. For me, it begins like a sprouting flower within my soul, and then it percolates into the expansiveness of my mind. It activates an internal "ring of truth," and I find myself nodding in agreement with each writer as a result. A beautiful and sublime experience.

While every story in this book is a testament to a life that has been lived full-out, what I hope you take away is that you, too, have a story. It may be similar to a story you read here, or it may be very different. You might have gone through some scary and traumatic experiences, or perhaps your life was less stressful. The specifics of your life experiences are not as important as the gifts that you received by going through them. Life experiences provide a context from which personal *Gifts of Wisdom* emerge. And believe me, you have such gifts—*lots* of them!

The key to remember, my friend, is that wisdom is not reserved for a select few special people. It's available to everyone—without exception—including you. My invitation to you is to take a closer look at your life story. Consider and review some of the important (or at least memorable) events, and revel in the amazing gifts the universe brought to you through those events.

Write everything down!

Don't worry whether the words make sense; just let them flow onto your journal pages and then preserve them somewhere. After all, those words are coming to you from your soul, and they represent important landmarks on your unique journey. Who knows, maybe next week, or next month, or next year, you'll come back to that journal and imagine bringing your wisdom to a completely new audience. I sure hope so—I'd love to read your story!

In closing, let me say that while it may be difficult to define wisdom or to know whether you've achieved it, rest assured that everyone has access to it—all you have to do is devote the time to turn your attention inward—toward your *MagnifEssence*.

To help you remember this, I offer the following inspirational quotes from past sages to give you additional guidance:

Keep me away from the wisdom which does not cry,
the philosophy which does not laugh and the greatness
which does not bow before children.
~ Kahlil Gibran

In the end, only three things matter:
how much you loved, how gently you lived,
and how gracefully you let go of things not meant for you.
~ Buddha

The greater danger for most of us
lies not in setting our aim too high and falling short;
but in setting our aim too low and achieving our mark.
~ Michelangelo

The man who asks a question is a fool for a minute;
the man who does not ask is a fool for life.
~ Confucius

It is the mark of an educated mind
to be able to entertain a thought without accepting it.
~ Aristotle

Knowledge is learning something every day.
Wisdom is letting go of something every day.
~ Zen Proverb

Until our paths cross again, my friend, I wish you boundless love, light, and blessings on your continuing journey. Stay loose and let the laughter (and wisdom) flow!

David D McLeod

Your Life Mastery Coach

Meridian, Idaho

About David D McLeod

Fighter pilot. Best-selling author. Software engineer. Mentor. Aerobics instructor. Poet. Janitor. Lifeguard. Musician. Radio host. Graphics designer. Father. Student. Teacher. Photographer. Ordained minister. Yogi.

These roles—past and present—add up to a *LOT* of life experience, which David D McLeod brings to bear in his capacity as a transformational speaker, life-mastery coach, experiential facilitator, and writer/storyteller.

As a Certified Master Life Coach and ordained minister with a PhD in Metaphysical Sciences and a DD in Holistic Personal Coaching, David creates and shares powerful *Life Mastery Tools* that enable adult men and women to transcend triggers, challenges and obstacles so that they can express and experience the fullness of who they really are and thereby manifest truly magnificent and fulfilling lives.

Visit David's Websites

- Your Life Mastery Coach: https://bit.ly/DDM-YLMC
- Life Mastery TV: https://bit.ly/DDM-LMTV
- MagnifEssence Life Mastery School: https://bit.ly/DDM-Mag
- Original Music: https://bit.ly/DDM-Music

Follow David on Social Media

- Facebook: https://bit.ly/DDM-FB
- YouTube: https://bit.ly/DDM-YT
- Twitter/X: https://bit.ly/DDM-X
- LinkedIn: https://bit.ly/DDM-LI
- Pinterest: https://bit.ly/DDM-Pinterest
- Amazon Author Page: https://bit.ly/DDM-Author-Page
- Wellness Universe: https://bit.ly/DDM-WU-Profile

Deep Gratitude

A book like this one does not come into being but with the loving support of many people who resonate with its vision and encourage its message to be shared with the whole world. I express deep gratitude to all of the following angels:

OMnitude, my boundless connection to *All-That-Is*, who—as the ultimate Source of all my so-called wisdom—guides my thoughts, words, actions, and emotions and keeps me fully aligned with my spiritual purpose for being;

Laura Di Franco, our fearless publisher and guardian angel, for her amazing skill at helping all of the writers discover and reveal their best selves within the stories they shared;

The entire team at Brave Healer Productions for the heroic efforts they went through to "herd the cats" and coordinate all of the writing so that everything was ready on time;

The design team, led by Dino Marino, that worked hard to produce an exquisite front cover and ensure the interior looked absolutely fabulous;

The intrepid readers who reviewed advance copies of the book and offered incredibly touching and insightful reviews for inclusion within these pages;

The entire launch team, whose dedication and enthusiasm helped spread the word, increase awareness of this book, and propel us toward bestseller status;

My brilliant author team, all of whom shared themselves openly and vulnerably in order to provide unique insights, wisdom, and experiences in a tapestry of profound healing and empowerment. It is through their voices that *Gifts of Wisdom* comes alive, offering a diverse array of practices and perspectives that inspire growth and transformation;

And last—but certainly not least—my wonderful readers, without whom this book would find no audience to appreciate it. It is you, dear reader, who makes this book worthwhile. May you find common ground in the stories and gentle healing in the practices.

WHAT'S NEXT?

BONUS RESOURCES FOR READERS

Gifts of Wisdom: Practices for Healing and Empowerment is much more than the simple book you have in your hands. Yes, in these pages you receive incredibly touching stories from brilliant authors who have shared some of the most vulnerable episodes in their lives. And yes, in these pages, you also receive powerful and intentional practices that can help you heal old wounds and empower you to tap into your own inner wisdom.

The gifts within this book are amazing indeed. But you may be looking for something more. Perhaps you'd like to deepen your experience with the material by connecting with some of the authors directly. Perhaps you'd like to receive personal guidance targeted toward one of your own challenging issues.

Of course, you can reach out to any of the authors directly by reading through his or her bio and visiting any of the resource links provided there.

But I have some very special news for you!

We have put together a collection of bonus resource offers in a centralized location. All of the participating authors have created highly targeted processes that will give you the opportunity to experience first-hand connection with them—and receive expert guidance and support in the bargain. To find out more about these offerings, head over to this page:

https://bit.ly/DDM-GOW-Bonus

Gifts of Wisdom BONUS
(Scan with your SmartPhone Camera)

COMPANION MUSIC ALBUM

I have another offer for you as well. If you enjoy ambient electronic music with a trancey meditative character, then you'll love the companion music album I created. I was inspired by the idea of wisdom and decided to write some music to capture some of my inspiration. This album is perfect as ambient background music to put you in a relaxed frame of mind for reading the contents of the book. You can access my album here:

https://bit.ly/DDM-GOW-Album

Gifts of Wisdom ALBUM
(Scan with your SmartPhone Camera)

SPECIAL OFFER

Receive 25% off by using this discount code:

gow#launch#special

Valid until December 31st, 2024, so don't delay!

ALSO BY DAVID D MCLEOD

A Conspiracy of Mirrors: Selected Poems; David McLeod; Outskirts Press, Inc.; June 2011

A Life to Die For: Master 10 Key Skills to Transform Your Life into a Priceless Treasure; David D McLeod; DreamSculpt Books and Media; June 2019

The Wellness Universe Guide to Complete Self-Care: 25 Tools for Stress Relief; Anna Pereira, Lead Author; Brave Healer Productions; November 2020

The Wellness Universe Guide to Complete Self-Care: 25 Tools for Happiness; Anna Pereira, Lead Author; Brave Healer Productions; January 2021

The Wellness Universe Guide to Complete Self-Care: 25 Tools to Achieve Anything; Anna Pereira, Lead Author; Brave Healer Productions; June 2021

The Wellness Universe Guide to Complete Self-Care: 25 Tools for Goddesses; Anna Pereira, Lead Author; Brave Healer Productions; November 2021

Find Your Voice, Save Your Life, Vol 4: Transcendent Men, Real Stories; Dianna Leeder & Scott Holmes, Lead Authors; Brave Healer Productions; August 2022

100 Poems and Possibilities for Healing; Laura Di Franco, Lead Author; Brave Healer Productions; January 2024

Follow David on his Amazon Author Page: https://bit.ly/DDM-Author-Page

www.ingramcontent.com/pod-product-compliance
Lightning Source LLC
Chambersburg PA
CBHW061144120626
46546CB00005B/1925

9 781961 493391